D1521205

Perilous Encounters

Commentaries on the evolution, art and science of medicine from ancient to modern times

Stanley M. Aronson, M.D.

authorHOUSE®

AuthorHouse™
1663 Liberty Drive
Bloomington, IN 47403
www.authorhouse.com
Phone: 1-800-839-8640

First published by AuthorHouse 9/11/2009

ISBN: 978-1-4490-2442-0 (sc)

Library of Congress Control Number: 2009909094

Printed in the United States of America
Bloomington, Indiana

This book is printed on acid-free paper.

Dr. Stanley M. Aronson

Foreward

For more than a decade, Dr. Stanley M. Aronson's *Medical Arts'* commentaries have graced the pages of *The Rhode Island Jewish Voice & Herald* with wisdom, humor and a compelling humanity.

This compilation of Dr. Aronson's columns will take readers on a journey into the history, heroes, marvels and maladies of ancient and current medical practices, captured in engaging tales. These range from Jewish Nobel Prize winners, to Biblical and medical giants – from Goliath to Maimonides – as well as notables from the Rhode Island Jewish medical community.

While many readers may be familiar with Dr. Aronson's academic, medical and research accomplishments, foremost as the founding dean of Brown University's medical school, his columns offer further glimpses of this erudite scholar and humanitarian, now 87.

He has lived a long and full life. Born in Brooklyn to immigrant parents, he attended a vocational high school where he once considered a career in carpentry as the only option open to him. In the depths of the Great Depression, however, he attended City College of New York, and was profoundly awakened to the world of intellectual inquiry. He majored in mathematics and marine biology, intent on a research career at the Marine Biological Laboratories on Cape Cod. But then came the attack on Pearl Harbor and the entry of the United States into World War ll; and with many of his contemporaries, he volunteered for the U.S. Army, serving in the infantry.

Years later, under the G.I. Bill of Rights, he attended medical school at New York University. His graduate training was in the neurosciences, as resident physician and fellow at a series of hospitals including Bellevue, Memorial Hospital for Cancer and Mt. Sinai. In 1952, he joined the medical faculty at Columbia University. Two years later, he began a 17-year career at the State University of N.Y., Downstate Medical Center, where he conducted clinical and laboratory research in degenerative brain diseases and was the author of over 400 scientific articles and six text books.

In 1970, Dr. Aronson was recruited by Brown University and founded its medical school in 1972, serving as its dean until 1981. He then reverted to student status, earning a graduate degree in public health at Harvard University and has since continued to teach at Brown. In these years he has found time to begin and lead Rhode Island's Hospice Care program as well as the Interfaith Health Care Ministries, edit the state medical journal, write a weekly newspaper column and work overseas for the Rockefeller Foundation.

I served as Dr. Aronson's editor for five years and now have the happy task of editing this collection of commentaries. His earlier columns were edited by the former managing editor of the newspaper, Jonathan Rubin, and the former editor of *The Jewish Voice*, the late Jane Sprague. I know I speak for them when I say what a pleasure it has been for all of us to work with Dr. Aronson.

This publication would not have come to fruition without the support of the newspaper's publisher, The Jewish Federation of R.I.; its editorial board, as well as the newspaper's generous patrons.

Mary Korr
May, 2009

Table of Contents

Chapter 7

Chapter 1

The Book: A manual to overcome the wilderness

Imagine an ancient confederation of tribes fleeing from Egyptian bondage and now struggling to sustain themselves in the wastelands of Sinai. They are landless, and in their hasty departure they salvage few things of enduring worth, nothing much more than their families, their flocks, their resolute leadership and their religion.

Leviticus, the third book, begins with a call from the Lord to Moses enjoining him to instruct the Israelites in matters of survival...

Imagine now the many problems which this tribal cluster must confront as it faces the challenges of nomadic life in a hostile desert: the ideological schisms, the pervasive doubts about their faith, the anomie which inevitably fragments a wandering people, the bewilderments, the unexpected encounters with hostile tribes, and the absence of any clear timetables or goals.

Imagine too, the periodic hungers, the inexplicable diseases, the lack of health care resources, the unending sense of impermanence, and imagine, finally, the personal agonies of those burdened with the leadership of this stiff-necked band of unenfranchised farmers, shepherds and artisans involuntarily made to roam by evil circumstance.

What terrible anxieties must have lingered, night after night, in the minds of Moses, Aaron and the tribal leadership. Beyond rudimentary survival, what ambitions, what goals, might have occupied their thinking? While no written agenda has survived, even a casual reading of the five books of Moses reveals a primal determination to preserve their monotheistic set of beliefs in the face of competing polytheisms;

1

a need ultimately to find a safe haven, a sanctuary after the decades of wandering in the wilderness; a fierce desire to maintain their identity, and above all, a pledge to keep the tribes in good health so that the aspirations of the elders of Israel might be achieved.

Exodus, the second book of the Holy Scriptures, tells the story of the Israelite departure from Egypt. The tribes are now isolated in the desert, no longer beholden to an alien power. They must now learn to survive in a hostile environment and, in the absence of an established social structure, learn to govern themselves.

Leviticus, the third book, begins with a call from the Lord to Moses enjoining him to instruct the Israelites in matters of survival: instructions concerning sacrificial offerings, the range of priestly duties, the determination of guilt and the nature of suitable punishment, charity ("when you reap the harvest of your land"), the defining of trespass, the acts of purification, the distinction between the sacred and the profane, the foods which are acceptable and those which are an abomination ("He shall not eat anything that died or was torn by beasts."), that which is clean and that which is unclean, diseases which may be contained and those which demand quarantine, the atonements of Aaron, the rules of civil behavior and the implacable nature of the laws of the Lord.

When read through current eyes, Leviticus appears to be a roster of prescriptive laws, many harsh and inflexible, perhaps even intolerant. It regards those with physical deformity, for example, as unworthy of active participation within the holy precincts. It relegates those with birth deformities, at best, to a secondary role in ritual activities. But this book is not some idle homiletic, some recitation of canonicals for the 20th century faithful. Leviticus was assembled for a nomadic population striving for survival, a group of wanderers some 29 centuries ago seeking stability and eventual nationhood.

The Mosaic code offered in Leviticus is an astonishing set of sensible, far-reaching regulations which did much to preserve the health and integrity of an imperiled people through numberless generations. It talks intelligently of the essentiality of cleanliness, of the many hygienic uses of water, of the disposal of waste ("Do not contaminate the earth where ye live for I dwell there also"), of the infectivity of certain diseases, of the hygienic care of clothing, of diagnostic criteria for various skin and venereal diseases. Leviticus provides an early model in rational preventive medicine.

Leviticus offers little in the way of tribal history or genealogy and less of the poetic majesty which makes the Bible such a singular document. It has neither the music of the Psalms, the wisdom of Solomon, the passion of Isaiah, the remonstrances of Jeremiah, the insight of the prophets, nor the anguish of Job. It reads more like an army instructional manual than a learned commentary. Yet this book of some 27 legislative chapters is an extraordinary document. It recognizes the maturation, painfully achieved, of the Israelites and declares, in essence, that the desert is an unforgiving merciless place with little room for mistakes or permissive attitudes. For these tribes to survive, there must be rules carefully adhered to, and these rules governing the health of its members are as critical to their survival as the most basic of religious principles. Disregard of the health rules in the nomadic camp becomes a heresy, and cleanliness emerges as a companion of godliness.

Numerous pastoral tribes have traversed the deserts of the Middle East, some defeated in battle, some absorbed by larger tribes, some succumbing to unknown fates, most losing whatever identity they had originally possessed. One tribe which wandered the trackless Sinai over two millennia ago did not disappear from history. They were aided in their survival by a set of pragmatic rules ("by the pursuit of which man shall live") which sustained their faith, their identity and their well being.

And they were counted, one by one

The second book of the Torah contains a brief passage in which the Lord instructs Moses to conduct a census of the Israelites (Exodus 30:11-16). This time-consuming accounting was undertaken, explains the text, to allow every person to pay the Lord a ransom and in so doing protect each of them against the many plagues. The gathered funds were to be used to maintain the tabernacle and its inner sanctuary.

And why, to this day, do Jews persist in counting their number?

There is no further mention of a census until the fourth Book of Moses, called Numbers, which begins with these words: "On the first day of the second month, in the second year following the exodus from the land of Egypt, the Lord spoke to Moses in the wilderness of Sinai, in the Tent of Meeting, saying: Take a census of the whole Israelite community by the clans of its ancestral houses, listing by names, every male, head by head...all those who are able to bear arms." This command was issued at an unsettled time when the landless Israelites were confronting the harshness of desert life, scarcity of water and food, attacks by hostile tribes, inner dissensions and regressions and the uncertainties of the future. Why then did these nomadic tribes devote precious resources to a frivolous dalliance such as the determination of their demographic profile?

The most obvious reason was the compelling need to count and then organize the younger adult males into 12 units for the defense of the Israelite multitude which numbered, according to the Bible, 603,550 men, women and children.

Many of the remaining chapters in Numbers are devoted to detailed instructions to Aaron on the care of the altar and sanctuary, the actions of some restive Israelites whose rebellion included the honoring of Moabite gods; appropriate altar sacrifices, the line of march through the deserts of Sinai, the laws of inheritance and finally the selection of Joshua, son of Nun, as successor to Moses.

Yet it remains a curious reality that the first ordinance provided to the Israelites in this book, and the basis for its name, was the numbering of its people. In no other heroic recountings of the wanderings of peoples, in preserved texts such as the Viking sagas, the *Odyssey* or the *Aeneid*, does one encounter this demand for such quantification, for the singular act of determining how many, of what gender and of what age.

And why this second census but two years after the first? Why, in the unfriendly wilderness where mere survival was the paramount consideration, did they bother to count people? For military purposes primarily, but also for public health planning, to define genealogy and the future equitable distribution of land, to initiate a tradition, to reinforce a covenant and thus to forge an ethnic identity. Millennia later, the scholar Rashi commented: "Because of the love of them is before Him, He counts them every hour; when they went out of Egypt he counted them, and when they transgressed with the golden calf he counted them."

In some non-Jewish traditions there exists a conscious hostility toward counting. Knowing the number or even the personal name of a group was to capture its essence. In some cultures it is taboo to count friends, so children in the course of their games will count, not one, not two, not three, etc.

And why, to this day, do Jews persist in counting their number? They render an account of themselves because Jews are not some anonymous multitude but a community of distinct individuals brought together by heritage and common purpose. Counting therefore bears witness to their comings and goings, their births, their deaths, as well as an appraisal of their needs. How many infants and children, and are their nutritional and health needs fulfilled? How many orphans, and does the Jewish community meet their needs? How many refugees, and are their wants addressed in terms of education, medical and basic living requirements? And for the elderly, what is needed in the way of assisted living, nursing homes and congenial shelters for those with dementia?

About a decade ago, two nationally known demographers, professors of sociology at Brown, undertook a major survey of the Jews of Rhode Island. Drs. Calvin Goldscheider and Sidney Goldstein completed a detailed social and demographic survey of the Jewish community. Their massive report, some 412 pages in length, discussed in precise detail the resident Jewish population (by age, gender, income, geographic location, education, etc.), migrational patterns, living arrangements and households, education and occupational achievements, religious identity and synagogue participation, Jewish networks, community service and charitable enterprises and even data on the extent and ramifications of intermarriage.

This expertly undertaken inquiry confirmed that the Rhode Island Jewish community was declining in numbers (in 1963, 19,700 Jews in 5,930 households; in 1987, 17,025 Jews in 7,224 households); intermarriage had become more frequent with generations of fewer children, and was composed increasingly of elderly and infirm, many living alone. Was this the prelude to the assimilation and collapse of the Rhode Island Jewish community, or, rather, was this the emergence of a numerically shrinking but nonetheless vibrant, affluent, well-educated, stable and influential society bearing smaller numbers of children yet providing each of them with greater sustenance, love and access to the best of educational resources? Certainly these Jewish children exceed their parents in educational and occupational accomplishment. Is smaller sometimes better? It depends on one's point of view. Some may curse the thorns on a rose bush; others will rejoice when roses bloom on a thorn-bush.

The ancient tradition of counting the Israelites flourishes in current Rhode Island; and as a result the community may now allocate its resources for health, education and the care of the disadvantaged in a rational manner. Jews count simply because each person truly counts.

The mysterious affliction of Miriam

In the fourth book of Moses, called Numbers, there is a brief, enigmatic story describing Miriam's affliction. The nomadic Israelites are about to depart from the desert village of Hazeroth on their wearisome trek through the wilderness of Paran. Miriam and Aaron, overwrought because of their brother, Moses, who had married a Cushite woman, spoke against Moses, exclaiming: "Has the Lord spoken only through Moses? Has He not spoken through us as well?"

Incensed, the Lord appeared as a pillar of cloud and admonished Moses, Aaron and Miriam, declaring that only His servant, Moses, may speak directly with the Lord. And as the divine cloud dissipated, Aaron and Moses beheld with horror that Miriam was suddenly stricken with snow-white scales over her body. Both Moses and Aaron then prayed to be forgiven for their many follies and said: "Let not Miriam be as one dead." The Lord replied: "Let her be shut out of camp for seven days, and then let her be admitted."

And as the divine cloud dissipated, Aaron and Moses beheld with horror that Miriam was suddenly stricken with snow-white scales over her body.

In the second book of Chronicles there is an account of the lengthy incumbency of Uzziah, king of Judah. During the late years of his reign, however, he grew arrogant and usurped the altar functions of the Aaronite priests. Azariah, a courageous priest from Jerusalem, then confronted the king; and Uzziah, before the eyes of the gathered temple priests, suddenly developed leprosy. The king was forthwith isolated as a leper for the remainder of his days.

What was the nature of Miriam's skin disease? Was it, as with King Uzziah, divine retribution for the wages of arrogance?

The 13th chapter of Leviticus provides a detailed description of a skin ailment, called leprosy, often with snow-white patches. ("As for the person with a leprous affection, his clothes shall be rent, his head shall be left bare, and he shall cover over his upper lip; and he shall call out,

'Unclean! Unclean!' He shall be unclean as long as the disease is on him. Being unclean, he shall dwell apart; his dwelling shall be outside the camp." (Leviticus 13:45-46).

Even if the scaly disease with white patches, called *tzara'ath* in Leviticus, is the same as contemporary leprosy, it is still unlikely that Miriam's acute affliction was leprosy. But the larger question presents itself: Was this a skin disease of human proportion, such as tuberculosis? Or, was it rather a manifestation of divine displeasure expressed metaphorically in a form that humans might understand? In so many instances, the biblical leprosy followed acts of human arrogance, idolatry, blasphemy or abuse of power. And the Bible, for all of its insights, is not a reliable source of medical information.

Ptolemy II (309-247 BCE), ruler of Egypt, commissioned 70 Jewish scholars to translate the Hebrew Bible into Greek. This version, called the Septuagint Bible, has formed the basis for virtually all subsequent biblical translations and exegeses. When these scholars encountered the Hebrew word, *tzara'ath*, they used a Greek word meaning scaliness (*lepra*). And it was later presumed by those who gave names to human diseases that the biblical leprosy was the same as the chronic skin and peripheral nerve disorder prevalent in the Middle Ages.

In truth, leprosy is a slowly evolving, chronic disease, minimally contagious and grossly disfiguring only if neglected for lengthy intervals. It is caused by a bacterium first described by Armauer Hansen. (Leprosy is now a rare disease in the United States; but when encountered, physicians call it Hansen's disease, thus removing the social stigma attached to the word leprosy.) Patients with Hansen's disease are treated in general hospitals since there is no need for them to be segregated from others. Worldwide, there are about 10 to 15 million people with Hansen's disease.

If the word, leprosy, is ignored for the moment, and if the disease of Leviticus is compared with the affliction currently called Hansen's disease, there is little resemblance. The Scriptural disease may have been a contagion which no longer exists. Or, alternatively, it may have been a form of infectious skin disorder superimposed upon a dietary deficiency such as pellagra.

There is little doubt that a secular disease called leprosy did exist in the Middle Ages and that church leaders then uncritically burdened its victims with the harsh injunctions described in Leviticus. By the 13th century, lepers were seen as bearers of a loathsome disease occasioned by a moral sin, a disease condemned above all other afflictions in the Scriptures. They were forbidden to live close to mortals, to enter into any commerce or otherwise commune with mankind; they were deprived of the right of church attendance (although allowed to watch church services by peering through narrow slits in the church walls) and were not permitted burial within consecrated churchyards.

But lepers were also declared to be blessed outcasts and given shelter without fee in special Lazar houses scattered throughout Western Europe. The corruption of the flesh was already assumed and the declared purpose of these sanctuaries, therefore, was to achieve salvation of the soul rather than the body.

Leprosy was the only disease for which contemporary society demanded permanent quarantine, in essence, life imprisonment. A relentless mythology has caused incalculable pain and suffering for those sufferers unfortunate enough to contract a bacterial disease which bore some remote resemblance to an affliction described in Leviticus.

Such laws also existed in the United States until the middle decades of the 20th century. Leprosariums were established in such places as Carville, Louisiana, and the Hawaiian island of Molokai, segregating by law the sufferers of Hansen's disease. Only through the insistence of the medical profession have the victims of Hansen's disease been recently freed from these barbaric restrictions.

Miriam's affliction lasted but a week, and then there was no further mention of it. At least two questions arise: First, what was the nature of her brief disease - an arcane form of leprosy, perhaps? And second, why was Miriam punished while Aaron was not?

He ate no bread and drank no water

As a volitional act, fasting has probably preoccupied humans as long as they have believed in the redemptive capacities of self-denial.

Not until Exodus, however, is there Scriptural mention of fasting. From the "Wilderness of Sin" the Israelite community paused at Rephidim and then encamped before a mountain in

In later years, fasting became a vehicle for social protest (as with the hunger strikes of Mahatma Gandhi and others).

Sinai. Moses ascended this mountain to hear the instructions from the Lord. "And he was there with the Lord forty days and forty nights; he ate no bread and drank no water; and he wrote down on the tablets the terms of the covenant, the Ten Commandments." (Exodus 34:28).

Voluntary fasting was not a sane choice for those primitive hunter-gatherer societies where hunger loomed as a periodic threat to the continuity of their community. Societies at the margins of survival, particularly nomadic groups, showed little tolerance for fasting since the full energies of each adult were needed for group survival. Fasting, as a voluntary act, assumes ritual importance only when there is a reasonable abundance of food and when credible choices may therefore be made. A chronically hungry man will rarely think of fasting voluntarily. On the other hand, in the words of St. Jerome, "When the stomach is full, it is easy to talk of fasting."

However, it was Moses huddled on Mount Sinai's summit and not the Israelites who first abstained from eating. Only later does Leviticus speak of an enduring obligation for all Israelites. "And this shall be to you a law for all time: In the seventh month, on the tenth day of the month, you shall practice self-denial; and you shall do no manner of work, neither the citizen nor the alien who resides among you. For on this day atonement shall be made for you to cleanse you of all your sins; you shall be clean before the Lord." (Leviticus 16:29, 30). And to reinforce the importance of this commandment, the instruction is repeated and amplified (Leviticus 23: 26-32) specifying now that the interlude of self-denial extend from evening to evening. But nowhere is abstention from food expressly mentioned; it is assumed to be one of a number of acts of self-denial appropriate to the Day of Atonement.

The Bible mentions the act of repentance; at other times, a mechanism by which secular distractions are purges to achieve communion with the spiritual world. Some times it is an ascetic act of humility, a renunciation of immediate pleasures so that ultimate enlightenment might be attained. In later years, fasting became a vehicle for social protest (as with the hunger strikes of Mahatma Gandhi and others).

Starvation, as a voluntary act, fulfills many functions. There are clear, fundamental differences, however, separating a hunger strike (undertaken to change something outside of oneself) and a fast (undertaken to change something within oneself). Over the centuries, fasting has been employed for diverse purposes, base and lofty, frivolous and thoughtful. In recent times, it has even been used when preparing patients for surgery or as a means of achieving weight reduction.

Philosophers recognize the following categories of fasting:

Purificatory fasting: Since eating may be viewed as a pleasurable act of self-indulgence, fasting may then be a way of tempering the base spirits, of suppressing vagrant and dissolute thoughts thus allowing loftier perceptions, sometimes called visions, to emerge. Daniel, in mourning, abstained from food and drink for three weeks and then, having practiced abstinence before the Lord, was confronted with oracular visions (Daniel 10:2, 3).

Physicians have documented many pathophysiological changes which accompany starvation. In addition to weight loss, loss of appetite, lassitude, weakness, ketosis and lowered blood pressure, victims may also experience euphoria and visual delusions.

Penitential fasting: As an act of remorse for specific sins, David acknowledged his evil ways before Nathan and then fasted when the health of his newborn son, by the wife of Uriah, was in great jeopardy (2 Samuel 12:23). Joel admonished the Israelite elders and priests to repent, to behold the devastation around them and then to make solemn their repentance by fasting (Joel 1:14).

Meritorious fasting: Fasting may be employed as a means of achieving a higher rank in life such as with the ritual fasts preceding knighthood or priesthood. Amongst the Crow Indians, each male youth must undergo a total fasting in the wilderness before his entrance into manhood is validated.

Disciplinary fasting: This is distinguishable from penitential fasting by two features: First it presumes the universal fallibility of humans; and second, it sets aside a specific time of the year, each year, as an interval for atonement through self-denial. By definition, it is a repetitive act in reaction to an unerringly corrupt, voluptuary world. Jews originally had one annual day of fasting. But during the Babylonian exile, four additional days of fasting were inserted into the religious calendar in remembrance of the siege and destruction of Jerusalem. And later, a day of fasting was proclaimed to recall Esther's fast. Muslims are enjoined by the Koran to accept neither food nor fluid from sunrise to sunset on each of the 30 days of the month of Ramadan. Early Christians were instructed to fast each Friday; but this obligation has been gradually modified over the centuries. In 1917, the *Codex Juris Canonici* required abstention only from animal flesh leading to the current custom of eating fish on Fridays.

When did fasting as a pathway to some higher goal, arise? When did a human decide that abstaining from food might gratify, or at least appease, his Creator? Did fasting come about, perhaps, in conjunction with the primitive practice of sacrificing food upon an altar? Was it a way of reinforcing the altar sacrifice by saying, "The food that I now sacrifice in Your honor was taken, not from some plentiful source, but from my very mouth, my meal. And as this lamb is sacrificed upon Your altar, so now do I sacrifice a part of myself by fasting."

And yet not all Scriptural commentaries considered fasting to be commendable. In a voice that is both prophetic and curiously modern, Isaiah declared that fasting, "a day for men to starve their bodies," can often be but an empty display of fealty to the Lord. A true fasting, said Isaiah, must be a time "to unlock fetters of wickedness, to let the oppressed go free, to share bread with the hungry and take the wretched poor into your home." (Isaiah 58:3-7).

The many travails of Esau

Genesis includes a number of stories describing conflict between brothers, even fratricide, but only one tale involving twins.

Rebekah, wife of Isaac, gives birth to two boys. The first to leave

Why was Esau so indifferent to, or careless of, his patrimony?

her womb, and hence the elder, is a newborn who is red all over, and because he is hairy she calls him Esau. His fraternal twin, younger by minutes and clinging to Esau's heel, has smooth skin and is called Jacob. They are indeed twins but yet are dramatically disparate in appearance and behavior. Esau, who maintains his excessive hairiness throughout life, becomes a skilled hunter "with the taste of meat in his mouth." He is much favored by his father, Isaac. Jacob, on the other had, is a mild man who confines himself to camp, and he is his mother's favorite.

We know nothing of their childhood or adolescence until a curious happening described without elaboration, in Genesis. Esau comes in from the fields and sees Jacob cooking a stew. "Give me some of that," he exclaims, "for I am famished." Jacob replies, "First sell me your birthright." And Esau declares, "I am at the point of death, so of what use is my birthright to me?" Jacob then gives him bread and lentil stew. Esau drinks, eats, and apparently now renewed in body, departs. And thus, through malevolency by one twin and negligent indifference by the other, is a perilous heritage traded for a mess of lentil porridge. With apparent casualness Esau spurns his birthright.

Questions now arise: Why was Esau so indifferent to, or careless of, his patrimony? Was he prone to reckless, impulsive behavior? Did he not care about his birthright, or might there exist a deeper reason for his seemingly nonchalant attitude? And other questions inevitably surface: Why did not Esau, by all descriptions an aggressive young man, debate the issue or at least bargain with his brother Jacob? Was his craving at that moment so uncontrollable that all other considerations were left in abeyance?

An enigmatic statement appears within the context of this brief story. Esau declares, "I am at the point of death." Genesis is not prone to hyperbole and Esau's exclamation must therefore be accepted as something more that a mere figure of speech.

Time passes, and Isaac, now elderly, becomes blind. He realizes that his allotted time is shrinking and he now calls for Esau so that he may bestow a final blessing upon his first-born. Isaac first asks Esau to hunt some game and prepare it as his favorite dish. Rebekah overhears this conversation and in secret instructs Jacob to deceive his father into thinking he is Esau. Rebekah even clothes Jacob's arms and neck with animal skins to simulate Esau's excessive hairiness. The ruse succeeds and a misled Isaac bestows his cherished blessing upon Jacob.

In time, Esau returns from the hunt and slowly comprehends the full dimensions of the duplicity. Trembling with anger he implores Isaac, "Bless me too;" the blessing to the wrong son, even though it was rendered under fraudulent circumstances, nonetheless cannot be reversed. Isaac says to Esau, "Yet by your sword shall you live." And Esau, with anger undiminished, "harbors a grudge against Jacob" and vows in time to kill him. Jacob flees to the encampment of his uncle, Laban. And Esau is not mentioned again until Jacob's lengthy interval of indentured labor has passed.

Years later the brothers are reunited in burying their father in the cave of Machpelah; and then there is no further mention of Esau; although, in subsequent years his descendants, the Edomites, are in frequent conflict with the Israelites, the descendants of Jacob.

And that is the way it was: An unheroic, disquieting narrative of two brothers, distinguished by appearance and behavior, their early years made notable by crass deception and enmity followed by decades of separation, and then a final reconciliation. The descendents of the twins, though, remain sworn enemies and fight many battles between the plains of Bethel and the mountains of Seir. Even in Rebekah's womb, the scriptural text tells us, the twin brothers fought.

Most fraternal twins resemble each other, but not Esau and Jacob. Might there have been a physiologic reason for their profound physical differences? And were there elements in this unadorned tale of Esau and Jacob to give credence to clinical speculation?

Esau, to an objective observer, may be described as follows: He is hyperactive as a fetus, and is born with excessive body hair (hypertrichosis) and with a redness of his body; as a youth, he is aggressive, a natural hunter, an eater of animal flesh. Endocrinologists have long associated these clinical features with a rare disorder of the newborn consisting of a pathological overgrowth of the adrenal glands.

Male infants with this uncommon disorder, called congenital adrenal hyperplasia, are encountered in about one in every 5,000 births. Such infants show enhanced virility, prematurely developed genitalia, aggressive behavior - and increased body hair. Professor Robert Greenblatt, an eminent endocrinologist, has pointed out that individuals with this glandular syndrome are also burdened with episodes of near collapse ("I am at the point of death.") when their body becomes periodically depleted of salts and the level of their blood sugar is dramatically reduced; and during such episodes they crave foods containing an abundance of salt and carbohydrates.

Were Esau's cravings, then, so compelling that he relinquished his precious birthright in order to bring his body metabolism back to a normal level? His fratricidal rage, of course, continued undiminished since his underlying glandular disorder was still operative.

The scriptural information regarding Esau, filtered through many translations and commentaries, is meager and surely inadequate to offer a plausible diagnosis. Furthermore, some may deplore a clinical scrutiny of these events as a blasphemous intrusion into a sacred text. Yet man has been given an inquiring spirit—some may say a prying mentality - to examine all things within his vision. And as scholars of language and theology examine the Torah word by word; as agronomists document each of the plants mentioned in the Bible; as archeologists turn over the soil of Israel in attempting to validate its past, so too may physicians ask the question: Did not human illness play some contributory role in shaping the destiny of the Israelites?

Laban's daughters and the essence of mandrake

In terse terms, Genesis tells of the complex relationships between Jacob and Laban's two daughters, Leah and Rachel, particularly in their intense desire to bear Jacob's children. At one critical point, Rachel declares, "Give me children, or I shall die." And later, at the time of the wheat harvest, Leah's son, Reuben, comes upon some mandrakes in the field which he gives to his mother. Rachel then implores Leah, "Please, give me some of your son's mandrake." (Genesis 30:14).

Why, in what seems to be an irrational demand, did Rachel beseech her sister to yield the mandrake herbs harvested by Reuben? Why, in a Scriptural book densely packed with critical historic recountings, is there even inclusion of a dialogue concerning an obscure herb?

Rachel, in her consuming need to overcome her barrenness, may have reflected upon a folk belief that small doses of mandrake had both a sedative and fertility-enhancing action. One doesn't study the Torah to learn pharmacology, but even in ancient Scriptural texts one encounters enigmatic hints explainable only by assuming that the pastoral Hebrews had some minimal acquaintance with herbal therapeutics.

Mandrake was certainly known to the Greeks. They called it *mandragos*, a name which over the centuries was corrupted to its current form of mandrake. It was a name historically associated with magical events; and, even in the 20th century, when a comic book magician needed an historically sanctioned name, Mandrake was an obvious choice.

The plant itself, a biennial native to the Mediterranean basin, is a rather ugly thing with fetid, fleshy leaves and clusters of berries. The roots (where the pharmacologically active substances are concentrated) have a characteristic fork-shape which, with some vivid imagination, may be said to resemble the human form. The legend arose, then, that each mandrake plant imprisoned a small demon. Certainly when someone imprudently chewed the mandrake roots, he quickly became wildly demented, paralyzed and often died.

Mandrake became an herb crucial to many tribal initiations and fertility ceremonies. In small doses it served as a calming sedative and was frequently given to those awaiting crucifixion.

By the Elizabethan era, mandrake was well-known for its effects as a tranquilizing agent. Shakespeare has Cleopatra say, "Give me to drink *mandragora*, that I might sleep out this great gap of time. My Anthony is away." And Shakespeare's Othello declares that poppy and mandrake are amongst the "drowsie syrups of the world."

It didn't take long for many to appreciate that dosage was critical: a little resulted in pleasant sedation, somewhat more to hallucinatory madness, and still more, led to death. John Donne appreciated the perilously narrow range between therapeutic and lethal concentrations of mandrake when he wrote, "...mingled wine with mandrake, whose operation is betwixt sleep and poison."

Linnaeus, the great classifier of plants, called it *Mandragora officinarium* (the mandrake of the apothecaries). He placed it in a large botanical family called the *Solanaceae*, a division which includes such diverse plants as the potato, the common tomato, pimento, tobacco, pepper, eggplant and even the petunia.

A 17th-century contingent of British soldiers, stationed in Virginia, once harvested a local plant called the Jamestown weed. They added it to their salad and within hours became wildly manic and disruptive. When they finally recovered they recalled little of what happened. The weed, now called Jimson Weed, is distributed widely throughout the United States and had been used extensively by the Aztecs as part of their sacrificial temple rites. Many Native American tribes of the Southwest continue to cultivate the weed (technically called *Datura stramonium*) for religious ceremonies. Datura intoxication causes headache, nausea and vomiting, intense thirst, dizziness and hallucinations; and if the dose is greater, is then followed by convulsions, blindness and death. Jimson Weed and mandrake contain similar psychoactive agents.

The most pharmacologically active of the solanaceous plants is commonly called deadly nightshade (*Atropa belladonna*). This plant yields atropine, a critically important drug in medicine and surgery. Related to atropine are the drugs hyoscine and scopolamine, sometimes called truth serum. (*Atropa* was the third of the three Grecian Fates held responsible, in legend, for determining the length and destiny of each person's life.) Historians say that the frenzied behavior characteristic of the ancient Bacchanalian rites of Greece was brought about by adding belladonna to the wine.

The older Greek legends, as embodied in Homer's Odyssey, tell the story of the mythic enchantress, Circe, who effectively used a decoction of *mandragora* to beguile and disarm the sailors of Ulysses. There is Homeric magic to this legend; and to say that the sailors were made compliant merely by a weak solution of scopolamine is to diminish the poetic power credited to the song of Circe.

The pharmacologically active plants of this botanical family (mandrake, *datura* and *atropa*), are globally distributed and share similar intoxicating and sedating alkaloids. No culture was ignorant of their neurophysiologic properties. (There is, however, no currently credible evidence that mandrake root enhances fertility.) Certainly these botanical agents have been regarded with awe and respect by native groups on every continent. It is naive, then, to presume that the ancient Hebrews, and in particular, Rachel, would have been totally ignorant of the powerful pharmacological effects attributed to mandrake root.

The *Solanaceae* provide humanity with an astonishing variety of products for food (potatoes, tomatoes, eggplant), for culinary enlivenment (peppers), for morbid diversion (tobacco), for beauty in the garden (petunias) and for medication (atropine, scopolamine). The effects of the medicinal herbs of this group upon humans were universally known, and, inevitably, some were mentioned in the Bible. But only when their pharmacological properties are appreciated could Rachel's compulsive demands for mandrake be understood. The authors of Genesis must have assumed that the effects of mandrake consumption were common knowledge; they therefore provided no further explanation for Rachel's urgent request.

Mania, melancholy and the falling sickness of ancient leaders

The Bible describes Saul as a deeply troubled monarch subject to spells of melancholy and intervals of manic behavior: "An evil spirit from God came mightily upon Saul." (I Samuel 19:9). There was an episode when he fell to the ground and lay there for both day and night.

Biblical scholars, including Dr. Julius Preuss, have interpreted these episodes to suggest that Saul was a victim of the falling sickness, currently known as epilepsy.

There is, in truth, no authentic description of epilepsy in the Hebrew Scriptures. Certainly it takes a substantial measure of imaginative credulity to accept the descriptions of Saul's distress as clear proof of his epileptic status. A skeptic, religiously observant or not, could offer many alternative reasons why Saul fell to the ground. It might have been fatigue, grief, remorse or even an overwhelming humility in the presence of a higher authority.

Some interpreters of the Bible also point to the description of Abram falling before the vision of the Lord (Genesis 17:3) as an example of an epileptic equivalent. The evidence is at best meager, as is the reference to Balaam when he saw the vision of the Lord (Numb. 24:4) "falling into a trance but having his eyes open." This is a frail bit of evidence upon which to hang a diagnosis of epilepsy.

Epilepsy is not that rare, and it is therefore curious that the Hebrew Bible provides no reliable description of the disease. There are few human diseases which arise so abruptly, speak so boldly, and define themselves so readily as epilepsy. There is little clinical subtlety when the major form of epilepsy descends upon its victim. The unbidden affliction announces itself explosively with altered consciousness (with the eyes usually remaining open), inarticulate cries, diminished motor control, convulsions and incontinence followed by an amnesic interval of variable length.

The early Greeks called it *Herakliea nosos*, the illness of Hercules, since the legendary hero had been prone to seizures. Ancient Rome was well acquainted with epilepsy. They called it *morbus caducus* (the falling sickness), *morbus sacer* (the sacred sickness), *morbus demoniacus* (the demonic sickness), or *morbus comitialis* (sickness of the assembly hall), since it was customary to shut down the public assembly site (*comitia*) for ritual purification whenever any Roman legislator experienced a seizure.

In Act 1, Scene 2 of Shakespeare's *Julius Caesar*, Casca recounts one of Caesar's many epileptic attacks: "He fell down in the market place, and foamed at the mouth, and was speechless." Brutus responds: "Tis very like he hath the falling sickness."

Chapter 9 of the Gospel according to Luke begins with Jesus assembling his 12 disciples, giving them "power and authority over all devils and to cure diseases." This story then unfolds: "And, behold, a man of the company cried out, saying, 'Master, I beseech thee, look upon my son, for he is my only child.' And lo, a spirit taketh him and he suddenly crieth out; and it teareth him that he foameth again, and bruising him hardly departeth from him. And I besought thy disciples to cast him out; and they could not."

It is a poignant story easily understood by any diligent parent. And it describes a disease that did not then respond to casual therapies. While many feared epilepsy as a demonic possession, rational voices were also heard. Hippocrates wrote that epilepsy was not a spirit-possessing disease but a disorder much like any other. "And they who first referred this disease to the gods, using the divinity as a pretext and screen of their inability to offer any assistance, have given out that the disease is sacred...Neither truly do I count it a worthy opinion to hold that the body of man is polluted by god."

Epilepsy seemed to have been so common amongst the leaders of antiquity (Caesar, Alexander the Great, even Caligula) that some thought it to be a necessary attribute for military greatness. Some feared and avoided the epileptic. Others believed that the seizures stemmed from a body occupied by divine sources; and accordingly the epileptic was often treated with respect, even homage.

A gradual transformation took place in the Medieval era when epilepsy increasingly was viewed as a manifestation of satanic possession and therefore required theological rather than medical intervention. John of Gaddesden, the famous English court physician of the 14th century, when confronted with an epileptic patient, advised that the physician whisper into the patient's ear: "Depart demon, and go forth!" He commented further: "This species of devil is not cast out save by prayer and fasting. The patient should then write out this gospel and wear it about his neck and he will be cured."

Before the 19th century, therapy for epilepsy varied from the bizarre to the ineffectually innocent. The blood of gladiators or executed criminals was frequently recommended as a preventive measure; and Hans Christian Andersen recalled seeing parents force their epileptic children to drink the warm blood of recently beheaded criminals. A standard anti-epileptic decoction in those days consisted of the boiled and macerated leaves of elder, garlic, peony and mistletoe. Why mistletoe? Because it tenaciously clung to the upper branches of the oak tree, never falling to the ground, and hence it must be helpful in the falling illness.

Gradually though, the neurophysiologists explored the nature of normal brain impulses and the manner in which certain segments of the cerebrum held dominion over motor activity in the four limbs.

Epilepsy was then conceived of as an explosive event in which ungoverned impulses were initiated from an abnormal cerebral locus. The idea of out-of-body possession was now replaced by the more secular concept of abnormal, involuntary excitation arising from a pathological segment of the cerebral cortex. And gradually, too, effective therapies, both medical and surgical, were devised.

Studies have demonstrated that there are many forms of epilepsy, not all convulsive, caused by a spectrum of unrelated ills including birth injury, vascular disorders, metabolic changes and even brain tumors. Current treatment has evolved to a stage where the great majority of epileptics may now lead productive lives unburdened by the threat of seizures. But society's memory is long, and there are those who still think of epilepsy as possession by demonic forces.

And the Lord put a mark upon Cain

The October 1991 newspapers carried the story of the discovery of a frozen body recovered from a mountain glacier situated between Italy and Austria. Archeologists determined that the body was about 5,000 years old. Careful examination of this Bronze Age human revealed numerous tattoos on his limbs and back. Tattooing instruments have also been recovered from a number of archeological sites in Europe indicating that the deliberate marking of the body by piercing the skin with needles carrying red and black dyes may date as far back as the Upper Paleolithic period (10,000 to 38,000 BCE).

Primitive humans, almost always male, often had indelible marks placed upon their bodies as visible evidence of their passage into adulthood, as symbols of having conquered some formidable beast, as signs of victory in some conflict or as membership in a particular clan. Tattooing was also used as a lasting stigma upon those ancient humans who were ostracized from the general community because of some criminal behavior. ("And the Lord put a mark upon Cain ..." (Genesis 4:15).

The Hebrews, to distinguish themselves from the heathen tribes that they had encountered during the exodus from Egypt, declared that body marks were to be prohibited. The Lord spoke to Moses, saying, "You shall not make any cuttings in your flesh or incise any marks on yourselves," (Leviticus 19:28); and later, "None shall defile himself" (Leviticus 21:5). Indeed, this injunction is repeated twice more in Deuteronomy. Yet there are scriptural scholars who believe that the Hebrews had practiced some sort of tattooing while in Egyptian bondage; but during their decades of wandering in the wilderness of Sinai these cultic rituals were gradually eliminated.

Tattooing is akin to body painting, a widespread primitive practice noted in virtually every culture. But while body paint denotes a willingness to enter into battle (as with the Picts) or to mourn the death of an elder, it remains nonetheless a temporary sign that can be readily washed away. Tattooing, on the other hand, is permanent and speaks of a lifelong commitment, evidence of a notable achievement or an expression of clan loyalty declared by those so marked. A painted face says that today I am a warrior. A tattooed chest says that I have been proclaimed, for always, to be an adult male, to be a proud member of a clan, to have passed through a painful initiation; and by virtue of these permanent marks, to have earned some mystical immunity protecting me from the hostile forces which surround me. The tattoo is my talisman, my good-luck charm. It will protect me.

The Romans employed tattooing largely for practical purposes. Their warriors proudly bore legion names and numbers upon their wrists; and Roman slaves were duly marked so that all would know the names of their owners as well as their indentured status.

In Western Europe, the migrant Celtic tribes practiced a primitive form of tattooing as did the non-Christian Norse. In the year 787, Pope Hadrian declared tattooing to be a barbaric practice and placed a ban upon it, although the Anglo-Saxon Christian warriors continued for centuries to mark themselves. During the Norman invasion of England in 1066 CE, the slain body of King Harold was identified on the battlefield of Hastings by his many distinguishing body marks. Tattooing lingered for a few more centuries in Christian Europe, largely confined to Scotland and a few Balkan enclaves.

Resumption of tattooing in the modern era began in 1770 when an avid English public read the vivid South Seas descriptions provided by Captain Cook. The narratives of his globe-girdling trip portrayed body tattooing as a widespread practice in virtually all Polynesian groups, particularly the New Zealand Maoris. In these newly encountered Pacific cultures, where body clothing was minimal, body marks announced one's clan membership, one's military record, one's fishing prowess and even one's profession. For the Polynesians, tattooing provided a visual resume for all to see. Even the word, tattoo, is from the Tahitian language.

A few of the captured Polynesians were brought back to England and duly exhibited in London. Some of the returning British mariners were also suitably tattooed; and for a while, tattooing was a sure sign of the sailor. A few members of the British royalty, more as an exotic act than a religious statement, allowed themselves to be so marked.

In America, tattooing was more aggressively pursued. During the Civil War it was customary for combatants on both sides to have their regimental symbols permanently displayed on their forearms. Tattooing remained a military idiosyncrasy, more so in the navy than the army.

During the Middle Ages, Jews continued their prohibition of any body marking. Indeed, Jewish physicians actively refrained from using any substance such as charcoal in the treatment of open wounds of the body, lest the carbon particles be absorbed into the interstices of the scar tissue and thus simulate a tattoo.

And to this day, for a variety of compelling reasons, Jews generally avoid tattoo marks upon themselves. What, for example, might a Jewish mother feel when seeing her teenage son's biceps adorned with a tattoo - even a tattoo dedicated to his mother? That he is permanently scarred? That he has abandoned Jewish values and is probably seeking companionship with the dispossessed, the chemically dependent and the vagrant motorcyclists of the nation? That he is about to leave home?

There are, indeed, tangible hazards other than the emotional or cosmetic, when one is tattooed. Tattooing consists of repeated, shallow needle-pricks facilitating the entrance of a permanent dye within the upper layers of the skin. Blood is sometimes drawn but not in significant amounts. The medical dangers of tattooing, therefore, rest in the inadvertent transfer of some pathogenic agent from one customer to the next, carried by a contaminated tattoo needle. The diseases capable of transfer by tattoo needles include syphilis, hepatitis and AIDS.

Tattooing may be an attractive undertaking for adolescents desperately seeking identification in some marginal group. But for Jews tattooing remains an obscene reminder of Birkenau-Auschwitz when prisoners had been involuntarily identified by tattooed numbers.

'Is there no balm in Gilead?'

Medicine, more than any of the worthy professions, has been identified as an intimate part of the Jewish temperament, character and heritage. Certainly there are many more Jewish school teachers or successful Jewish businessmen than Jewish physicians, but when the time comes to recount the Jewish heroes of the past, names such as Maimonides, Ehrlich, Salk and Sabin are the first to spring readily to mind.

Truth is sometimes difficult to establish. But when all else fails, it may occasionally be found hidden below the surface of the casual humor of the day. It is likely that there are more Jewish jokes containing the phrase, "My son, the doctor" than "my son, the architect" — or my "son, anything else." And despite all of the bitter changes that have corrupted the practice of medicine in recent years, "my son, the doctor" (or more commonly, now, "my daughter, the doctor") leads the wish-list of most young Jewish families.

But where in the three millennia since the exodus through the Sea of Reeds has this curious predilection for medicine arisen? And what in the collective experience of the Jews has led to this presumption of an intimate alliance, if not a marriage, between medicine and Judaism?

The earliest written judgments, priorities and regulations of the Hebrews are found in the Bible. And yet the Scriptural writings think quite disparagingly of the practice of medicine as well as those who call themselves physicians. Hosea says of Ephraim who had sent for a foreign physician: "He will never be able to cure you, will not heal you of your sores." (Hosea 5:13). "In the thirty-ninth year of his reign, Asa suffered from an acute foot ailment; but ill as he was, he still did not turn to the Lord but to physicians. And Asa slept with his fathers." (II Chronicles 16:12).

In his exasperation, Job says to the counselors and physicians, "But you invent lies; all of you are quacks. If you would only keep quiet it would be considered wisdom on your part." (Job 13:4, 5). And a despairing Jeremiah cries aloud: "Is there no balm in Gilead? Can

25

no physician be found? Why has healing not yet come to my poor people?"

Clearly, the physician, Hebrew or alien, was not a revered person in the ancient Hebrew community. Nowhere is the physician praised, thanked — or even acknowledged as a worthy member of the community. And in the case of Asa, third king of Judah, and his unidentified foot ailment, the Bible tells us in tactful words that he died shortly after his physician treated him ("And Asa slept with his fathers") as though this was the expected outcome of medical intervention in that time.

Given the primitive nature of clinical medicine in the Mosaic era, the skepticism and disdain regarding the physicians' curative capabilities is quite understandable. But if they had no faith in their practicing physicians, what then did these Hebrews believe in? First, they declared that while caring and nurturing were indeed human responsibilities, healing remained the province of the Lord. "See, then, that I, I am He; There is no god beside me. I deal death and give life; I wounded and I will heal." (Deuteronomy 32:39). Thus, the ancient Hebrews believed that both the causes as well as the cures of mortal illness stem from divine action. Given that reality, what could a mere mortal do?

Micah, the Morashtite, declared: "He has told you, O man, what is good, and what the Lord requires of you: Only to do justice and to love goodness, and to walk modestly with your God." But God-fearing men and women were also expected to provide food for themselves, create shelters against the elements, clothe themselves, nurture their children, shepherd their flocks, prune their vineyards and protect their communities. And early in their history as a coherent community they created and abided by a complex series of instructions, injunctions and prohibitions concerning the health of the public. Scholars note that there are 613 commandments and restrictions in the Torah; and 213 of these concern ways of protecting the health of the Hebrews.

These rules are explicit, unambiguous and assertive. There is, for example, no poetry in Deuteronomy 23:10-14; but here, thousands of years before the germ theory of diseases was proposed, are instructions concerning defecation while in the field and the need to preserve the cleanliness of the region. ("Let your camp be holy.") There is even a stated requirement that all Hebrew soldiers carry a shovel in their gear to cover their excrement.

The Pentateuch is replete with instructions on quarantining; on defining what is clean and what is unclean; on foods that may be consumed and foods that are prohibited; on the cleaning and disinfecting of clothes, objects brought into camp, and even on the fumigation of homes. The communicability of certain diseases is assumed and feasible steps needed to prevent the spread of disease are clearly outlined.

Leviticus, particularly, was a practical survival manual for the migrating Hebrew tribes as they negotiated a path through the wilderness of Sinai and beyond. The texts of Leviticus and Deuteronomy are filled with instructions concerning everything about human existence, from birth to illness to the proper way of burying the dead. Curative medicine may not have been praised in the Bible, but certainly preventive medicine was heavily emphasized. And thus, gradually, did the Hebrews come to understand that to sustain life they were also required to undertake such active measures that would prevent or lessen the likelihood of disease. And if preventive medicine was scripturally acceptable and did not deny the ultimate role of the Lord, might not curative medicine follow in time? Sophocles (495-405 BCE) declared: "Heaven helps not the man who will not act." And Benjamin Franklin (1706-1790) expressed it more positively: "God helps them that help themselves."

Physicians of the Biblical era then became tentative helpers in the healing process. (Said Ambroise Pare (1517-1590): "I treated him. God cured him.") And medicine, Jewish and non-Jewish, struggled to find interventions that would do more good than harm. Certain herbal extracts such as opium and digitalis were found to be effective. Cleanliness, advocated by the Torah but ignored by many until the 19th century, did much to suppress infectious disease; and only by the 20th century could medicine confidently claim to possess curative powers for many ailments.

Which still doesn't explain the continuing reverence directed by Jews toward the practitioners of medicine and the persistence of an intimacy between the practice of medicine and Judaism. It remains a puzzle to all but Jewish mothers.

What need have I for incense?

In the beginning there were animal sacrifices, made holier by the addition of aromatic substances. (The word, sacrifice, is derived from a Latin word, *sacrificium*, meaning to make holy or sacred.) This was replaced in time by burnt offerings of wheat and oil, again augmented by additions of fragrant substances such as frankincense; and still later by incense alone.

Boswellia thuringa, and related species, are scrawny, undistinguished, shrub-like trees confined to the remote and inhospitable hinterlands of the southwestern Arabian Peninsula, the savannahs of the Somali region of East Africa and the mountainous reaches of northern India. The tree yields neither blossom nor fruit of any worth; and its wood has little utility beyond impromptu bonfires. And were it not for the precious nature of its resinous sap, the tree would be virtually unknown.

When the bark of Boswellia tree is deeply gashed, either through some natural accident or by human intent, a gelatinous sap exudes which in time hardens into yellow, translucent, crystalline globules no bigger than small grapes. This drab-looking resinous substance, sought after by so many of the ancient civilizations of the Fertile Crescent, is now known by its Latin names, frankincense or *olibanum*, both terms derived from earlier Hebrew names. By tradition, the resinous globules have been hand-gathered, packed into sheepskin bags and shipped then by camel-train to the Middle East or by vessel to the spice markets of South Asia.

Frankincense resin is bitter to the taste, oily in texture and inflammable. Indeed, its central role in early Hebrew ritual, and its uninterrupted harvesting over the centuries, rested solely on its capacity to burn slowly, yielding a uniquely pleasant aroma.

The Torah talks of the need by the nomadic Hebrews to sanctify their tabernacle with an aroma pleasing to the Lord. Moses is instructed by the Lord in the procedure by which the altar-incense of the Tent of Meeting is to be prepared. "Take fragrant spices: gum resin, aromatic shell, *galbanum*; add pure frankincense to the spices in equal proportions." (Exod. 30:34). The frankincense was to be burned in the morning hours when the sanctuary lamps were trimmed and again in the evening hours when the lamps were again lighted (Exod. 30:7, 8).

The Queen of Sheba is said to have brought to Solomon's court a camel train laden with frankincense and other spices of exotic origin. Isaiah talks of camel caravans bearing precious spices and incense. Nehemiah speaks of frankincense as a substance so treasured that it was stored in the inner recesses of the great temple in Jerusalem (Neh. 13:5-9).

But the burning of precious incense, alone, was insufficient to sanctify either the site of praying or those in prayer. At a later time when His chosen people, now in exile, practiced abominations, the Lord declared: "For they would not hearken to My words, And they rejected My Instruction. What need have I for incense that comes form Sheba, Or fragrant cane from a distant land? Your burnt offerings are not acceptable and your sacrifices are not pleasing to me." (Jer. 6:19, 20). And in the Christian Bible, Matthew tells of the three wise men from the East, the magi, who traveled to the manger in Bethlehem bringing gifts of gold, frankincense and myrrh.

The words, incense, frankincense, fumigation and even perfume (*per fumum*) all find their roots in Latin words meaning to burn (*incendere, fumigare*). Anthropologists have speculated that animal sacrifice by fire had been an integral part of all primitive religious observances. And, to the participants, the ascending sacrificial smoke represented the rising to the heavens of their devout prayers.

Certainly the early Hebrews rejoiced when they smelled the aroma of the immolated animal: "I offer up fatlings to You, with the odor of burning rams; I sacrifice bulls and he-goats." (Psalm 66:15). Adding something sweetly smelling, such as the oils of frankincense, must have been a reinforcing element of their earnest devotion and their desire to please their Creator. In time, the barbaric animal sacrifice was replaced by burnt offerings of wheat and oil: "And the priest shall turn a token portion of it into smoke: some of the grits and oil, with all of the frankincense, as an offering by fire to the Lord." (Lev.2:16). And in the later psalms we hear the burnt offerings now confined solely to the incense: "Take my prayer as an offering of incense, My upraised hands as an evening sacrifice." (Psalms 141:2).

And He smote them with...*what?*

The Book of Samuel (5:6) describes a curious sequence of events: The Philistine armies have captured the Ark of God and have placed it in their heathen temple in Ashdod.

"The hand of the Lord lay heavy upon the Ashdodites, and He wrought havoc among them: He struck Ashdod and its territory with hemorrhoids."

The King James translation of the Bible uses the Old English word *emerods*, meaning multiple swellings (sites on the body unspecified), perhaps

Philistine priests, now calling their disaster a plague, resolve to return the Ark to the Israelites and to pay an indemnity consisting of "five golden hemorrhoids and five golden mice."

hemorrhagic in appearance. The word is the etymologic precursor of hemorrhoid. The Septuagint translation of I Samuel 5:6 additionally mentions swarms of mice invading Philistine ships and fields.

The first Scriptural mention of hemorrhoids is found in Deuteronomy (28:27), which lists the many calamities befalling those who do not faithfully observe the Lord's commandments: "The Lord will strike you with the Egyptian inflammation, with hemorrhoids, boil-scars and itch, from which you shall never recover."

The text in Samuel then recounts the subsequent distress among the Philistines and their fear that mere possession of the Ark will bring only calamity. The Ark is then hastily moved to a succession of Philistine communities, but the "panic of death pervaded the whole city, so heavy had the hand of God fallen there; and the men who did not die were stricken with hemorrhoids. The outcry of the city went up to heaven."

The story continues: Philistine priests, now calling their disaster a plague, resolve to return the Ark to the Israelites and to pay an indemnity consisting of "five golden hemorrhoids and five golden mice." The Philistines then place the Ark, with the golden objects, upon a cart driven by two milk cows that are allowed to wander. The cart, with its precious objects, enters the community of *Bet Shemesh*, where the people rejoice at the return of their precious Ark.

Beyond this text, there is no further mention of hemorrhoids in the Scriptures; one is therefore left with an improbable narrative that the punishment for such a monumental crime as the stealing of the Ark of the Covenant is something as clinically trivial as rectal hemorrhoids. Furthermore, unless hemorrhoids were a far more lethal disease in biblical times than they are today, it would not have caused men to die, cities to panic and destruction to be widespread. Priests, even Philistine priests, are stoical souls unlikely to be dismayed by a few cases of hemorrhoids.

Thus, we are confronted with a puzzle: The Philistines capture an object sacred to the Israelites; either as a consequence, or coincidentally, they are subject to a terrible affliction. What else is revealed to us? Their misfortune had a plague-like quality, spreading rapidly through the urban masses of Philistines. Furthermore, this mysterious infirmity seemed to be lethal, to such a degree that the militarily superior Philistines eagerly sought to rid themselves of their greatest trophy of war. And finally, there is the tangential mention of swarms of mice and golden statuettes of mice to be given as indemnity to appease the wrath of the Lord.

The word hemorrhoid, as currently used, has a narrowly defined meaning portraying passive enlargement, and occasional hemorrhaging, of perianal veins. It is a common disorder, rarely debilitating, not known to be lethal and certainly not communicable as a plague might be. The great etymologist and authority on biblical medicine, Dr. Julius Preuss, declares that the word should be translated as local swelling and is cognate with other Semitic words meaning illness-related enlargements.

Are there diseases endemic to Asia and the Middle East that might more closely fit the limited description afforded in Samuel? If the isolated scriptural hints are indeed relevant, the disease should have a high mortality rate, manifest itself clinically by surface swellings (perhaps hemorrhagic), associated in some fashion with swarms of rodents, and be so highly communicable as to create utter panic and governmental dismay.

There is such an infectious disease — of Asiatic origin and endemic to the Middle East for millennia: bubonic plague. It is caused by a bacterium (*Yersinia pestis*) and it is primarily a lethal disease of rodents, usually house rats. As an infected rat dies, its blood-sucking fleas (containing the germs of plague) seek other warm bodies to parasitize. Usually the fleas will find other rats to provide them with homes, but if there are humans nearby the infected fleas may choose them.

The ensuing disease is rapid and often lethal. One of the most distinguishing features of plague is the dramatic involvement of lymph nodes, causing them to enlarge to considerable size, forming swellings called buboes (hence the term, bubonic).

Historians have speculated on the nature of this Philistine plague. Many communicable diseases have been considered, but plague seems the most likely culprit.

Plague cast a singularly grim shadow upon the already perilous lives of 14th-century Jews. As bubonic plague spread north following its arrival in Italy in 1347, large numbers of Europeans succumbed; the survivors sought out those thought to have spread the plague, called the Black Death. Immense numbers of Jews were then accused of having caused the epidemic and were summarily burned at the stake.

Ironically, the bacteriologist who in the first decade of the 20th century first identified the causative germ of bubonic plague was Jewish.

The contentious boils of Job

The book that follows Proverbs in the Jewish Bible begins with these simple declarations: "There was a man in the land of Uz named Job. That man was blameless and upright; he feared God and shunned evil."

The Book tells us nothing of Job's lineage, ancestry or even his religion; and little is known of this strange place called Uz except for passing references to it in Genesis, Jeremiah, and in the sad poetry of Lamentations. But we know with absolute certainty that this man Job was a righteous and humble person. So righteous was he, in fact, that even the Lord praised him and took comfort in his piety. Satan then observes that piety is easy to experience when things are going well; and further, since Job is a fabulously wealthy person he can readily afford to be both pious and generous. Therefore, to prove that Job's abiding faith and reverential spirit are not merely the dividends of good fortune, God gives Satan permission to visit misfortune on Job.

Job's worldly goods are then wasted, his seven children are destroyed and he is reduced to an impoverished, calamity-ridden elder; his skin now covered from head to toe with boils. But, initially at least, Job does not blaspheme his Creator.

Why, in the scriptural story about the magisterial forces of good and evil, do we confront a rather banal infirmity called boils? Why did not Satan cast the misery of cancer or the loss of limbs, or even a devastating dementia upon the hapless Job? Possibly because the writer of this enduring metaphor on the quality of faith sought out a disease that was quick in onset, loathsome in appearance and would not deprive Job of his senses, his ability to express his anger and sacrilege or, alternatively, his abiding faith. And so, Job was afflicted with boils.

Boils are not that rare in the contemporary world and it must be presumed that they were visible afflictions also encountered in the post-exilic era when the Book of Job is thought to have been written.

Boils (skin abscesses) are most often seen in childhood as focal points of inflammation. The inciting germ is almost always in the staphylococcus family. Typically, boils form around an infected hair follicle or around some foreign object such as a splinter or a fragment of soil which has found its way below the skin. The skin is the most visible location for staphylococcus purulence. Staphylococcus germs are widely distributed in nature. With the advent of antibiotics and a more widespread appreciation of personal hygiene, the incidence of subcutaneous boils has greatly diminished except perhaps in adult diabetics.

But if you were to interview a random score of high school students, you might come away with a different impression. You would learn, for example, that facial boils and their precursors, the pimples, are more feared than a flu epidemic. Teenagers will watch, with a sense of horror, as these reddish pimples slowly enlarge, assuming sizes that convince them that they will momentarily be rejected by peers and relegated to the outer margins of high school society. These unaesthetic little outbreaks are referred to, generally in whispers, as "zits," the etymological origin of which is obscure.

Job, whose tribulations now included loss of health, family property and friends, finally berates God, declaring that his misfortunes are undeserved and even capriciously rendered. And in a debate of magisterial proportions, Job declares his insistence on arguing with God, but also bewails his miserable destiny. ("My bowels are in turmoil without respite. Days of misery confront me…I have become a brother to jackals…my skin, blackened, is peeling off me… my bones are charred by the heat.") At last does Job relinquish his pride and whisper, "I have heard You with my ears, but now I see You with my eyes. Therefore I recant and relent, being but dust and ashes." Job's wealth and status are then restored and the tale ends with these words, "So Job died, old and contented."

It was not the purpose of the author of the Book of Job to give its readership some notion of the diseases present during Job's days, nor their clinical features. It was sufficient merely to declare that the Lord's power extended beyond the number of cattle in his meadow, or the weight of gold in his treasury. It included dominion over the divine gift of health.

Chapter 2

Prognosis and prophesy in Medieval France

Gaul had been sparsely populated by Jews throughout the years of the Roman Republic but only as itinerant traders; there is no record of any permanent Jewish settlement in

> **We know him today by the name of Nostradamus.**

what is now France until the second century of the current era.

At that time Emperor Vespasian had permitted a small number of Jewish warriors, expelled from Judea, to populate the wilderness of Gaul. The residents of these rude enclaves were later jointed by more adventuresome civilian coreligionists from Italy and the eastern Mediterranean; and by the fourth century there were thriving Jewish communities centered in the Rhone River delta, particularly in established settlements such as Auvergne, Marseilles, Narbonne, Beziers and, especially, Montpellier. While these Jewish communities were largely agricultural they nonetheless contained the roots of mercantile enterprises including a thriving network involved in coastal commerce.

In general, these Jewish communities prevailed for centuries without molestation and had not been forced to migrate except during some of the early Visigoth invasions. In Narbonne, the synagogues totaled 300 congregants. A rabbinical academy flourished in Montpellier and there is documentary evidence that Jews were also locally engaged in the formal practice of medicine.

By the 13th century a combination of socioeconomic circumstances conspired to aggravate anti-Semitic sentiment and anti-Jewish legislation. Some of the riots and subsequent edicts seemed to have been provoked by unsubstantiated accusations that a Christian child had been ritually murdered.

In January, 1306, Philip IV ordered all Jews to leave France within 30 days. Many fled south to Provence, a temporary haven then under the jurisdiction of a Germanic prince. But the fervor and turmoil of the Crusades shattered any thoughts that southern France might become an asylum for the newly exiled Jews. By the 14th century the situation had deteriorated further and the remaining Jews of the southern provinces of Provence and Languedoc were then required to wear identifiable badges upon their outer clothing.

In 1381, following a succession of devastating bubonic plague outbreaks in lands south of the Rhine, there were renewed attacks upon the remaining Jewish communities of Europe; and those ancient Jewish communities near France's Mediterranean shores were decimated or destroyed. A French Jew, it was said, never slept without his shoes, cloak, and pilgrim's cane nearby. And in 1394 yet another formal expulsion of the skeletal Jewish communities of France was ordered.

But after each expulsion, and impelled solely by economic imperatives, the gentile rulers of France permitted some exiled Jewish families to return, typically under severe economic and civil constraints. No French Jew would find more than two generations of his ancestors buried in the same local cemetery.

It was during the winter of 1503, in the Rhone delta settlement of St. Remy, that a Jewish family gave birth to a son. The infant was named Michel and he later assumed the family name of Nostre Dame from the name of the district in which he was born. He grew to early manhood and was then sent north to the neighboring city of Avignon for university training in the liberal arts. Upon completion of his baccalaureate studies he traveled a short distance south to the university city of Montpellier, then the site of France's most illustrious medical school.

Four centuries before, Montpellier had established an independent academy of medicine, its early faculty composed largely of Jewish physicians. Towards the close of the 13th century, Pope Nicholas IV had the medical school incorporated into the local university.

The Montpellier medical faculty, during Michel's years of study, was justly renowned. It included the renegade cleric turned physician and satirist, Francois Rabelais, who supervised the seminars of the Aphorisms of Hippocrates as well as the established texts of Galen.

Upon graduation Michel entered the practice of medicine in Lyons. But somewhere during those early years of independent practice, the pressures of the Inquisition reached him and he then converted to Roman Catholicism. In 1534, he married and began a family. Tragically the recurrent bubonic plagues took the lives of his wife and children. He left France and for many years wandered extensively throughout Italy. Eventually, in 1554, he returned to France, remarried and settled in the town of Salon.

In addition to a prospering career in medicine, he began yet another venture: the writing of poetic quatrains, four-line poems each clustered in groups of one hundred called Centuries. In 1564, Michel was appointed as court physician to Charles IV, where his poetic fantasies were sought after as readily as his prescriptions.

On July 2, 1566, Michel de Nostredame died after a notable career as a diligent physician and healer. He lived an eventful 63 years, yet his enduring fame rests not upon his modest accomplishments as a physician. Rather his name persists because of the innumerable and enigmatic quatrains which he had composed. For centuries their cryptic messages have puzzled or bemused readers; some found them darkly portentous while others regarded them as innocent nonsense. To this day his rhymes are quoted - or misquoted - to convey the impression that he had been able to foresee the distant future with awesome clarity; and there are few present-day checkout counter publications that do not paraphrase his inscrutable quatrains in order to predict some impending calamity.

We know him today by the name of Nostradamus.

Two millennia of Jewish physicians in Italy

Most of the Judean rebellion had been crushed by the year of 68 CE, and Vespasian, called back to Rome to claim the laurel crown, left the final siege of encircled Jerusalem to his son, Titus. The walled city held out at great length but finally fell to the Roman legions. Of the Jews who survived, the strongest were shipped back to Rome in slavery.

These Judean slaves, of course, were not the first Jews to live on the Italian peninsula. There were small mercantile colonies of Jews in many Roman communities preceding other Jewish settlements in Europe. Indeed, despite periodic oppression and banishment there have been Jewish settlements in Italy, more or less continuously, for 22 centuries. During the reign of Augustus, census records indicate that there were about 8,000 Jews in Rome. (By 1965, the Jewish population in Italy was only about 34,000 or 0.1 percent of the population.) And Celsus, writing in the first century of the current era, mentions Jewish physicians and Jewish remedies.

There was an atmosphere of toleration toward the Jews of pagan Rome in the next three centuries. Jewish medicine flourished until the repressive edicts of Theodosius (438 CE). The chronicle of Jewish life in Italy for the next 15 centuries was a story of episodic tolerance and intolerance, oppression and relative freedom, banishment and permission to return.

Beginning with the reign of Pope Gregory I (590-604), the Jews of Rome and particularly their physicians, enjoyed much papal protection although this protection gradually had been eroded by numerous edicts requiring Jews, and infidels, to wear distinctive badges, live only in certain districts, and confine themselves to certain designated occupations.

Exceptions frequently were made for Jewish physicians. A Jewish doctor from Barcelona, Isaac Benevista, was appointed as court physician to Pope Honorius III in 1220. Some of the most eminent physicians of this era (Abraham ha-Rofe Anaw, Judah Romano, Hillel Ben Samuel and the respected Gajo) were Jews held in high esteem by the reigning popes.

Clearly, there was a notable difference between the words and the observance of papal edicts pertaining to Jews practicing medicine. The Synod of Valladolid (1322) acknowledged that prior prohibition on Jewish physicians had been given little attention. And even during the grievous years of the Black Plague in the 14th century, when Jews were blamed for the pestilence and many Jewish communities were destroyed, the Jewish physicians of the Papal States practiced without hindrance beyond the ghettos and were exempted from donning the red tabard marking the wearer as Israelite. Through the Renaissance, virtually every Pope included a Jewish physician in his entourage.

Historians have speculated as to why the Jewish physicians were so privileged. Certainly, as a group, they were well trained and dedicated to their art; typically they attended the medical schools of Salerno or Padua. Their immunity from oppression, it was conjectured, stemmed rather from the superstitious belief that magical skills can best be exercised by strangers, by outsiders, or those of alien faith. Furthermore, since antiquity, there had been a chronic shortage of trained physicians in Italy.

Many Jews sought haven in the Italian states during the late 15th-century Inquisition in Spain. Some communities, such as Livorno, then under the administration of the Medicis, actively invited them. Pope Alexander VI even chose a refugee physician, Jacob Ben Immanuel Provinciale (also rabbi to the Jews), to be his court physician.

Pope Paul III appointed Jacob Ben Samuel Mantino as his physician in 1534. State documents referred to him as Giacomo Ebreo (Jacob the Hebrew), while the Jewish community gave him the exalted title of *Gaon*, the Hebrew word for genius.

One of the more illustrious Jewish physicians of this century, Azariah Ben Moses dei Rossi (1513-1578), could trace his family back to the Hebrew captives brought to Rome by Titus. In this era, centers of Jewish medicine were known in Rome, Fano, Ferrara, Verona, Mantua and Venice.

The civil and mercantile liberties extended to Jews gradually declined during the pontificate of Paul IV. Jewish males were now obliged to wear a distinctive yellow cap and all Jews were required to live in the confining ghetto clinging to the shores of the Tiber River. At one point Jews were expelled from virtually all Italian communities except for the Papal States, Ancona and Livorno. A papal decree of 1729 confined Jewish commerce to rag and scrap metal collection. All these restrictions were removed when the French Republican armies occupied Rome in 1798, but were reintroduced when Napoleon was defeated. Yet, Jewish physicians continued their labors in both Jewish and Christian communities. Historians expressed the view that these Jewish physicians, by their skills, did much to sustain the fragile Jewish communities during the Medieval and Renaissance centuries. The Italian ghetto finally was destroyed in 1848. Some remnant of the unique esteem bestowed by Jews upon medicine must have persisted. During the last three decades two Jewish physicians of Italian origin have been awarded the Nobel Prize in Medicine: Salvatore Luria, born in Turin, for his work with viruses; and Rita Levi-Montalcini, also born in Turin, for her work in cell growth.

Maimonides: Physician-rabbi

Photo by Mary Korr

Sculpture of Maimonides in Cordoba, Spain, his birthplace.

Maimonides:
The physician-rabbi who cared for Saladin

At birth they named him Moses ben Maimon, son of Maimon ben Joseph, eminent physician and scholar; to those close to him, he was called Maimudi; to later generations of Talmudic scholars he was Rabbi Moses ben Maimon, but was more often referred to by his acronym, Rambam; and to Europeans, he was simply Maimonides, the great medieval philosopher and physician.

The widely quoted declaration by Maimonides that "a bastard who is a scholar takes precedence over an ignorant priest" did not sit well with some of his colleagues.

Maimonides was born in Cordoba, Spain, during the spring of 1135, into a family of noted scholars and judges. His early education, leading to secure a role as physician, was managed personally by his father. The relative tranquility in Cordoba was shattered in 1148 when the city was invaded by an army of militant Moroccan Berbers called the Almohads, an Islamic sect said to be "aflame with orthodoxy." Churches and synagogues were promptly demolished while residents not of the Islamic faith were given the choice of conversion or exile. For the next decade the family of Maimonides wandered in North Africa, finally settling in the Moroccan city of Fez, where they nominally adopted the Islamic faith as a means of survival. The Almohad dynasty left a heritage of religious intolerance in Spain but also an impressive architectural imprint, sometimes called Moorish, best exemplified by the Alcazar palace in Toledo. In 1212, the Almohads were decisively defeated by the Christian armies led by Alfonso I of Aragon.

In the year 1165, living circumstances in Fez became intolerable and Maimonides undertook a perilous voyage east to Palestine, then to Alexandria, and finally to Cairo where he lived and worked for the remainder of his productive life.

His medical skills became widely known in Egypt and within a few years of his arrival he was summoned to the court of Saladin to assume the role of physician, particularly for Saladin's son and heir, Nur-ud-din Ali. The large Jewish community of Cairo selected Maimonides as *Nagid*, their spiritual leader and spokesman.

His increasing prominence in Cairo, however, did not protect Maimonides from charges of apostasy. An Islamic judge asserted that he had converted to Islam while living in Fez and that he had then deserted his adopted faith. Only intervention by higher authorities prevented his summary execution.

In the decade which followed, the years in which he was most productive, a cascade of texts poured from his pen. During these golden years he translated much of the works of Hippocrates, Avicenna and al-Razi, interpolating his own clinical views in a manner similar to the accretive commentaries of the Talmud. Many of his books, particularly his amplifications of Galen's texts, were translated to Latin and read widely in Europe as *Dixit Rabbi Moyses*. His other medical contributions during this 10-year interval included books on sexual hygiene (written at the behest of Saladin's son), and treatises on such widely disparate subjects as asthma, poisonings, diets and hemorrhoids. Maimonides is also remembered as the author of an enduring compendium of medications, largely of botanical origin, patterned on the classical treatise of medications written a millennium earlier by Dioscorides.

Maimonides was regarded by his contemporary religious scholars as the equal of Rashi. Many of his coreligionists, however, despaired of his Aristotelian thinking and his emphasis upon reason. The widely quoted declaration by Maimonides that "a bastard who is a scholar takes precedence over an ignorant priest" did not sit well with some of his colleagues. Certainly his books were widely read, and just as widely disputed. His first great treatise on Torah exegesis was called *Book of the Lamp*, followed in a few years by his monumental inquiry into the five books of Moses (*Mishneh Torah*); and in the year 1190, the culminating text of his scholarly career, a book still read avidly today, called *Guide to the Perplexed*.

In a dark age when nonconformist speculation was akin to heresy, during an era sometimes called the Age of Faith, Maimonides proclaimed the merit of independent, critical thinking. "Since reason was implanted by God in man it cannot be contrary to God's revelation." He rejected astrology outright and insisted that certain testament passages must be interpreted figuratively since, in his judgment, they represented metaphors rather than inflexible realities. He denied the concepts of individual immortality, resurrection, anthropomorphic perceptions of God and disparaged notions of corporeal paradise.

Civil authorities grew increasing intolerant of Maimonides and his many unorthodox views. By 1191, Saladin was involved in a deadly struggle with the Crusader armies of Western Europe. The permissive atmosphere which had prevailed in Cairo was now replaced by a heightened Islamic fundamentalism. Prudence forced Maimonides to diminish his social and philosophic writings and devote more of his time to the practice of medicine.

In an 1199 letter, a Talmudic scholar had asked Maimonides that they spend time in discoursing on certain problematic religious tracts. Maimonides denied the request, stating that he now was committed to his clinical responsibilities. His typical day began at the court in Cairo, where he provided medical care for the immediate members of Saladin's family, their children and the inhabitants of the various court harems. He then returned late in the day to confront an antechamber filled with patients and supplicants. After washing he then ate his sole meal of the day. And then he examined a succession of patients well into the night until, with the antechamber finally empty, he fell exhausted to his bed to arise at dawn to repeat his daily agenda. Only on the Sabbath did he forswear medicine and lead the local congregation in services and Torah studies. Burdened by a relentless schedule and abetted by the inevitable anxieties of living in an alien society, Maimonides aged rapidly and died in 1204, his 69th year. His body was lovingly transported to Tiberias where it was entombed within a grove of trees bordering upon the shores of the Kinneret.

During a time when medicine, and indeed all science, advanced little, he is remembered as one of the great, rational physicians and philosophers of his age. He was a staunch advocate of reason, of moderation and, above all, of compassion. "Let me ever behold in the afflicted and suffering only the human being," he declared.

The Jewish physicians of Providence, when seeking a name for their organization, called it the Maimonides Society as a token of profound respect for the unique contributions of Rabbi Moses ben Maimon and the immortality of his ideas.

A dwelling set apart

The idea of a hospital as a place to arrest or cure disease has evolved slowly. Indeed, the first known hospital with this avowed purpose was established only within the last millennium.

Little is known about the earliest of dwellings set apart for the Jewish sick. The word "Bethesda," meaning a house of mercy, may have been such an ancient refuge.

The primitive home, residence for the extended family, provided an adequate location for all of the usual functions of daily life: a place to eat, sleep, work and educate children; a place to give birth; a refuge for the injured and ailing; an altar site for prayer to household gods, and a place to die.

Gradually, as increasingly co-dependent families merged into clans and clans into tribes, some of these domestic functions were relegated to jointly held, communal structures. Factories, at some distance from the home, replaced cottage industries; children were educated in central facilities; and at some point in the distant past, a decision was reached to remove a sick family member to a place other than home. This decision may have been motivated by compassion; or, more likely, out of fear that whatever possessed the sick person may spread to the healthy. In more primitive cultures, removing a sick member meant abandonment to the forces of nature.

When the nomadic Israelites were forced to confront leprosy, believing the disease to be communicable, they realized the need for some form of physical separation. They chose an alternative more humane than frank abandonment. "He shall be unclean as long as the disease is on him. Being unclean, he shall dwell apart; his dwelling shall be outside the camp." (Leviticus 13:46). And thus some form of dwelling "outside of the camp" was designated as a place for those deemed sick or unclean.

At a time when there was little distinction between the weary, the infirm, the insane, the elderly or the injured, maintaining a refuge for rest and nourishment became yet another function of the tribe. Accordingly, two forms of shelter gradually arose: one for the victims of contagion, such as leprosy, who were ostracized more to protect the community than to benefit the patient, and another as a haven for those incapable of functioning within the community.

There had been, of course, hospitals in Rome (called *valetudinaria*) but they served only injured soldiers from the Roman army. And there were temples of healing in many Asian and Mediterranean cultures, but their activities had been more spiritual than medicinal. The Council of Nicaea convened by Constantine in 325 CE demanded the closure of all such pagan temples within the jurisdiction of Rome. But the Council also urged that religious orders provide comparable shelters for the sick and weary.

These asylums had dual missions: as shelters for the pilgrim and havens for the sick. And two words defined their purposes: hotel and hospital. (Both words are derived from the Latin, *hospes,* meaning guest.) To this day many francophone hospitals are named *Hotel Dieu* (House of God). The institutions for the segregation of lepers, called *lazarettos,* also flourished. By the 13th century there were an estimated 16,000 leprosaria in Europe.

Little is known about the earliest of dwellings set apart for the Jewish sick. The word "Bethesda," meaning a house of mercy, may have been such an ancient refuge.

Visiting the sick was an ancient obligation of the Jews. The Israelite, in addition, was expected to acknowledge the needs of others. "You shall not abhor an Edomite, for he is your kinsman. You shall not abhor an Egyptian, for you were a stranger in his land." (Deut. 23:8). And if visiting the sick was a moral covenant for groups such as the *Bikhur Cholim* then it required but a small additional step for them to also bring food and medicines, and eventually to offer shelter.

The Hebrew word *hekdesh* defined a medieval community refuge for the Jewish sick where comfort, food in accordance with dietary laws, and simple medications were provided. At first the *hekdesh* might have been designed for all who were afflicted; but gradually its purpose narrowed to provide shelter solely for the destitute and terminally ill. As such, they deteriorated to little more than wretched places of last resort. The *hekdesh* persisted, at least in the Pale of Eastern Europe, until the 18th century. A Yiddish proverb of that era expressed the disparaging thoughts concerning this institution: *"Besser fruher starben in der heim, eider auf der after in hekdesh."*

The German city of Cologne seems to have had a general hospital for Jews in the year 1248. At least some state documents mention a *"Domus Hospitale Judaeorum."* Further Jewish hospitals are mentioned in Munich (1381), Trier (1422), Ulm (1499) and Berlin (1550).

The Portuguese Jews of London founded their own hospital in 1747, and in 1753 the Jews of Berlin had constructed a new hospital. Paris had its first Jewish hospital in 1836 and other European cities with sizable Jewish populations followed suit in the 19th century.

The Jewish population of the 19th-century United States, prompted in part by the indifferent and insensitive public attitudes toward Jewish sick, assigned funds to establish Jewish-operated hospitals. In New York City, the Jews' Hospital was constructed in 1852 (later called Mount Sinai Hospital); this was followed by a similar facility in Philadelphia (1864) and in Baltimore (1866).

In 1854, the Rothschild family of Paris resolved to alleviate the abject poverty and rampant disease of the Jews living in Palestine. This was a region plagued by endemic cholera, malaria, trachoma and other tropical and subtropical diseases. A small 18-bed hospital was then built on the side of Mount Zion, in Jerusalem, near the Temple Mount. This unit was enlarged in the early 20th century and moved to Mount Scopus where, with the inspired help of the founders of the Hadassah movement, a magnificent new hospital was opened. This hospital, now situated in Ein Kerem, has become the teaching facility for the Hebrew University faculty of medicine.

The historic advancement from the Biblical dwellings set apart for lepers to the present-day Jewish medical centers did not progress smoothly.

A Jewish shelter, a few millennia ago, had little to offer beyond a warm bed, culturally acceptable foods, and perhaps some rudimentary medicines. Indeed, many in the rabbinate regarded any medical intervention as sacrilege. They subscribed to the belief, supported in Scripture, that healing could come only from a higher authority.

It has required millennia for the hospital to mature from a hovel of despair to a place of hope; and now to a technological site where cure is commonplace. The religious orientation of such institutions, whether Jewish or Christian, has diminished appreciably. A Jewish "presence" in a hospital is now confined to its major financial donors, many of its health providers, *mezuzahs* on the doorways, Judaica in the gift shops and perhaps a name such as Beth Israel over its entranceway.

Medical education and its Jewish roots

For most physicians, medical education represents a life-long undertaking beginning in early adulthood and continuing until retirement.

Two Jewish physicians accompanied Columbus on his inaugural voyage in 1492.

While there had been academies in ancient Greece for the teaching of medicine, (often incorporated within the temple communities of Apollo or Aesclapius), the vast majority of physicians, until the current era, learned their art and science through apprenticeships. Medicine was a cult or guild rather than a science.

Before an academy or apprenticeship could call itself a medical school, it had to meet certain criteria, including a defined set of entrance requirements, a visible and defensible curriculum, and a resident faculty to teach and to certify that each candidate had successfully completed the stipulated course of study. Further, a medical school differs from an apprenticeship by offering a faculty of scholars, each one an expert in some component of the art of medicine, rather than one preceptor.

History identifies the Italian seaport of Salerno as the site of Europe's first true medical school. Salerno had been the site of a Benedictine abbey and hospice for the care of pilgrims and lepers. In many ways 10th-century Salerno had also been the intellectual crossroads of several divergent Mediterranean cultures, and was influenced by Roman, Hellenic, Arabic and Jewish philosophies.

The medical school at Salerno claims to have begun in the intellectual convergence of these four cultures, which for a short interval flourished in southern Italy with neither secular nor clerical hindrance. Historians say that each of the cultures was represented on the inaugural medical faculty at Salerno, although most of the instructors were said to be Jewish emigrants from the medical academies of the Middle East.

The Salerno school of medicine flourished for over a century although it sadly lacked instruction in the basic medical sciences. The students learned their anatomy, for example, by studying Galen's text on the internal morphology of the pig. In 1194, Salerno was sacked by mercenaries of the German King Henry VI and much of the medical school was destroyed. By the beginning of the 13th century newer Italian medical schools established in Bologna, Padua, Palermo and Naples, as well as in some southern French cities such as Montpellier, were attracting students from the far corners of Europe. Salerno continued to function as a medical school but its academic luster had diminished appreciably and only its famous compendium, *Regimen Sanitatis Saleritanum*, the standard therapeutic text for virtually every European medical school, persisted as a reminder of Salerno's former greatness. In 1811, after a thousand years of educating physicians, an order of Napoleon finally closed its doors.

During the 9th through 12th centuries, there were no Eurasian centers for medical education which were visibly Jewish, other than Salerno and Montpellier. The great medical advances of the Middle Ages consisted mainly in exploiting the forgotten texts of the classical world, including the works of Galen, Dioscorides, Aristotle and Hippocrates. The resurrection of these noble texts was largely due to the labors of Muslim physicians trained in the caliphates of southern Spain, northwestern Africa, Cairo and Baghdad.

By the 10th century, Baghdad had emerged as the great center for the study and advancement of clinical medicine, attracting physicians from the Persian clinics.

Spain, under the caliphate, also witnessed a blossoming of medicine. From Cordova came the famous Rabbi Moshe ben Maimon, known as Maimonides, who was later chosen to be Saladin's principal medical advisor.

Numerous Jewish physicians, trained in the Islamic medical centers of Spain, Baghdad and Egypt, were recruited to serve in the distant regions of the Muslim world, including parts of southern Italy and Sicily where Arabic influence had taken root. Jewish physicians authored numerous scholarly texts on pharmacological agents, diet and the principles of hygiene.

Until the Inquisition precluded further Jewish participation in academic medicine, Jewish physicians were prominent in the courts of Spain and Portugal, including Joseph Vecinho, the Portuguese king's personal doctor. Other Jewish doctors included Zemah Duran, an authority on gynecologic disease, who was later obliged to flee the Iberian peninsula to seek refuge in Algiers. Two Jewish physicians accompanied Columbus on his inaugural voyage in 1492. Rabelais and Nostradamus were educated at the medical school at Montpellier in southern France. Here, too, the earliest recorded clinical teachers were Jewish physicians. But as the school was given sanction by the church, the role of Jewish physicians as teachers diminished drastically.

The Inquisition, beginning in the late decades of the 15th century, drove most Jewish physicians back to the ghettos. There is little mention of Jews in the faculty rosters of European medical schools, or indeed in any scientific domain, until the 19th century when the Napoleonic emancipations allowed Jewish scholars to resume a meaningful role in the clinics, medical schools and the emerging research laboratories of Europe.

Chapter 3
Hospital named for latter-day Moses

It was said of him that his Creator had expressly provided him with a long life so that he might accomplish great deeds on behalf of his coreligionists. And indeed during his 101 years of productive existence, Moses Haim Montefiore became an extraordinary philanthropist, a supplicant for numberless Jewish causes, and an effective spokesman before sultans, beys, kings and tsars.

On the occasion of Montefiore's centennial birthday most Jewish communities on both sides of the Atlantic sought to honor this devout philanthropist.

Montefiore (Italian, hill of flowers) was born in Leghorn, Italy, in 1874 and migrated to London as a youth. He achieved great success as a stockbroker, amassing such great wealth that he was able to retire at age 43, devoting the remainder of his life to negotiating with heads of state on behalf of Jews who were unjustly imprisoned or deprived of certain basic rights.

His countless travels took him to Palestine, Russia, the Vatican, Morocco and numerous other sites where Jews were in need of his intervention. His family traveled with him as did his personal friend and physician, the great Dr. Thomas Hodgkin. (Hodgkin, a devout Quaker, had been one of England's leading physicians and had provided the description of what is now called Hodgkin's disease.)

In time, Montefiore became the most prominent Jew of the 19th century and was knighted by Queen Victoria. On the occasion of

Montefiore's centennial birthday most Jewish communities on both sides of the Atlantic sought to honor this devout philanthropist.

The leaders of the New York Jewish community, almost all of German or Sephardic origin, met on the evening of Feb. 4, 1884 in the vestry of Congregation of Shearith Israel to ponder ways by which their community might also immortalize the blessed name of Montefiore. Some advocated that a Jewish reformatory be established to house unruly young Jews stemming from the impoverished East European immigrants newly arrived in New York City. Still others, deploring the crowded tenements of Manhattan's Lower East Side, urged that new and spacious housing be specifically constructed for these coreligionists from Russia.

After weeks of intense debate, the organizing committee finally approved a plan to establish an institution for the delivery of health care. Mt. Sinai Hospital had been effectively operating on the East Side of Manhattan for decades as an acute hospital and therefore a different type of health facility was envisioned. The planners conceived of a haven for those whose disabilities placed them beyond the skills and capabilities of the conventional hospitals of the day, a congenial residence for those suffering from incurable diseases such as tuberculosis, syphilis, advanced arthritis, kidney disease, "the opium habit" and chronic melancholy. The social architects of this contemplated institution would offer clean accommodations, compassionate nursing, food in accordance with dietary laws, skilled medical care, rabbinical presence and full visitation rights for the families. Initially it was to be called The Montefiore Home for the Incurables but this ungainly name was soon changed to The Montefiore Home for Chronic Invalids. It would house 26 beds.

The trustees of the home rented an unpretentious three-story clapboard house on the northeast corner of East 84th and Avenue A, a house with a broad veranda so that residents might have protected access to the fresh air. On Oct. 19, 1884, the home admitted its first patient, a 30-year-old house painter suffering from painter's colic (chronic lead poisoning) and advanced pulmonary tuberculosis.

The local newspaper, the *New York World*, reported on Oct. 26th, "In all the synagogues throughout the city the Hebrews celebrated the 100th birthday of their noble leader in benevolence." Temple Emanu-El was packed on that day and the principal speaker honoring Montefiore was the eminent Rev. Henry Ward Beecher. A congratulatory cablegram was duly sent to Montefiore, then living in Ramsgate, England, announcing the opening of the home.

Chief of the medical services at the Home was Dr. Simon Baruch, born in Schersenz, Prussia in 1840 but educated at the Medical College of Virginia and a veteran, twice captured, of the Confederate Army. After the Civil War, Baruch migrated north from South Carolina and went on to become one of New York's leading public health physicians. He was the father of Bernard Baruch, advisor to many presidents.

Moses Montefiore was not to reach his 101st birthday. He died on July 28, 1885 and the residents of the Home bearing his name said *Kaddish* for a month.

By 1887, the trustees declared the Home to be non-sectarian but the institution nonetheless continue to serve principally the indigent Jews of New York. The Jewish population of the city, in three decades, had grown from 30,000 to 1.1 million, many of whom were in desperate need of medical services. The Montefiore Home now expanded, both in size and in the diversity of its services. In 1909, it moved to newly constructed inpatient and research facilities in the north Bronx. And by the latter decades of the 20th century, it has become a sprawling institution of some 2,000 beds, with a house staff of close to 600 and is the major clinical teaching facility of the Albert Einstein College of Medicine.

In 114 years, the institution honoring the great Moses Montefiore has evolved from a modest 26-bed home for the chronically disabled to a socially conscious hospital and now to an internationally renowned medical center, the core facility of a thriving college of medicine. In the words of one historian, "This was an institution where missions were interpreted broadly; where taking care of the family of the immigrant tailor was as important as taking care of his lungs; where doctors though it was important to go out to the slums and prisons in search of patients."

Truly, Montefiore Medical Center, a compassionate and communally responsible institution, fulfilled the dreams of its visionary founders when they sought to create a place that would match the beneficence of Moses Montefiore.

Amidst New York City turmoil, Jews created Mt. Sinai

The year was 1852 and Millard Fillmore presided over an expanding nation of about 24 million people. New York City, the nation's leading metropolis with a population of 500,000, was the site of severe unemployment, labor turmoil, soaring food pries and rampant currency speculation.

The Jews of New York, numbering perhaps 10,000, collectively believed

> *The new institution was called The Jews' Hospital. No fees were charged. ("No person should be allowed to die because he could not afford to live.")*

that there was an urgent need for a Jewish community hospital, partly to offer a kosher environment when their coreligionists required hospitalization, and partly because of a long-standing moral commitment that they continued to observe. A few Jews had been allowed to settle in Manhattan in the 17th century under the terms of the New Amsterdam Act of Toleration which specified that their residence was permitted provided they cared for their poor, orphaned, disabled and dying.

The Hebrew Benevolent Society of New York, in its meeting of Feb. 16, 1851, voted to establish "an Asylum for the Aged and Sick of the Hebrew persuasion." Donations had been solicited and a total of $1,034.16 gathered for an envisioned structure of some four stories. It was estimated that the total construction cost would approximate $10,000. A Manhattan site was chosen on West 28th St. between 7th and 8th Avenues. Before construction had begun a major gift of $20,000 was received from Judah Touro, late of Rhode Island, a bachelor merchant then residing in New Orleans. This act of immense generosity allowed the planners to incorporate such luxuries as gas illumination and indoor plumbing (with access to running water on all four floors). The planned bed capacity was increased to 45.

There were few hospitals in the New York of 1852. New York Hospital, a private institution supported by the Anglican Church, was constructed in 1771. The Sisters of Charity established a second private hospital, now called St. Vincent's Hospital, in 1849, and the municipal government maintained a few outpatient institutions, notably Bellevue Hospital on the island of Manhattan, and Charity Hospital on an island in the East River. Near Charity Hospital (later renamed City Hospital) the authorities also maintained a small plague facility (called the pest house) for patients with highly contagious disorders such as cholera or plague. The decision by the Hebrew Benevolent Society to construct and maintain a new hospital was therefore a bold undertaking. The Jews constituted, after all, only about 2 percent of the city's population.

The new institution was called The Jews' Hospital. No fees were charged. ("No person should be allowed to die because he could not afford to live.") In its first year of operation it admitted, free, 216 patients. If the 45 beds were constantly occupied, this indicated that the average length of stay, per patient, was about 76 days.

In an effort to go beyond sectarian needs, the new hospital opened its doors to non-Jewish patients, and its staff of attending physicians included many leaders in American medicine who were not Jewish (e.g. Valentine Mott, M.D., America's leading surgeon of the 19th century; Benjamin McCready, M.D., founder of the Belleview Medical School and a leading authority on occupational medicine, and Willard Parker, M.D., whose later efforts on behalf of public health led to the creation of a New York hospital named in his honor.)

In 1862, The Jews' Hospital was commandeered by the U.S. Army to care for the wounded soldiers of the Union Army and was continued as a military facility through 1866. The draft riots of 1863 had turned the streets of New York into sites of pitched battles and again the beds of The Jews' Hospital were employed to care for the injured. By the end of the Civil War the bed capacity of the institution had risen to 69. In 1866, the board of trustees voted to change its name to Mount Sinai Hospital of New York. The change of name served to emphasize that its core purpose was to provide medical service without distinction to race or religion, but without obscuring its Jewish roots.

The so-called Irish Riots of 1870 convinced the trustees that a much larger institution was needed. Accordingly, plans were being begun for a new hospital. A site was chosen at the northern outskirts of urban settlements in Manhattan, on Lexington Avenue between East 66th and East 67th Sts. On May 29, 1872, the new Mount Sinai Hospital was opened. It was an elegant structure of brick and marble, four stories high, with 120 inpatient beds in four pavilions. Its staff included a German refugee named Dr. Abraham Jacobi, later to become the country's leading pediatrician, and on its fulltime staff were two women physicians, Dr. Ann Angell and Dr. Mary Putnam Jacobi. A third woman physician, Dr. Eliza Phelps, headed the hospital's apothecary department.

The hospital established the first pediatric department in the United States in 1878 with funds donated by a Western merchant named Michael Reese. And in the same year an outpatient department was constructed to serve the indigent of the upper Manhattan communities. Mount Sinai Hospital became accessible to a much larger urban population when the steam-driven elevated railroad on 3rd Avenue extended its line, establishing its northern terminus at the 67th Street entrance to the hospital.

The Miriam: A Jewish Hospital

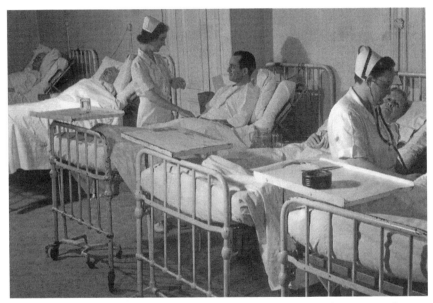

Photo: R.I. Jewish Historical Assn.

Patient ward at The Miriam Hospital in its early days.

What makes a hospital Jewish?

Is there a single attribute, a *sine qua non*, which identifies a health care institution as indisputably Jewish? For example, is a hospital necessarily Jewish if it is named for a prominent Jew? Is it Jewish if it bears a hallowed name such as Mount Sinai? Is it Jewish if it had been originally established by 19th-century Jews to provide medical coverage for their immigrant coreligionists? Is it Jewish if the medical staff is largely Jewish? Is it Jewish if the principal donors and trustees are Jewish? Is it Jewish if the majority of its patients are Jewish? The answer to these seven questions is an emphatic, "maybe."

What, prior to 1940, defined a hospital as Jewish? Certainly the entrance lobby of many older Jewish institutions conveyed an unmistakably sectarian message, with prominently displayed bronze plaques listing donors, visible bas-relief Stars of David and menorahs. Nearby was a small synagogue, and in the basement a kosher kitchen. The great majority of the patients were Jewish, and an intern was at a disadvantage if he could not speak elementary Yiddish.

Today, inner-city demographics have changed and only a fraction of patients treated in the urban Jewish hospitals are Jewish. (At Beth Israel in New York, the figure is less that 18 percent. And where this hospital had once employed a cadre of Yiddish interpreters, it now hires Spanish and Cambodian translators.)

There are a number of non-sectarian hospitals which bear Jewish names but are not, and never were, Jewish. Most of the municipal hospitals of New York carry geographic names, but two are named for past Jewish physicians: Goldwater Memorial Hospital is named for Dr. S.S. Goldwater, a physician-pioneer in hospital design and management. In the Bronx, the large general hospital adjacent to the Einstein College of Medicine is called the Abraham Jacobi Hospital, named for the great 19th-century physician and social reformer who had been chief pediatrician at Mt. Sinai Hospital. There is a number of major community hospitals in southern states named after Jewish industrialists who had donated large sums. The bestowed monies apparently carry no sectarian stipulations.

The Touro Infirmary in New Orleans, the General Rose Memorial Hospital in Denver and the Michael Reese Medical Center in Chicago, all named for eminent Jews in American history, are now nonsectarian. In fact, the Touro Infirmary's original documents stipulate that it treat all peoples, including blacks.

The names given to most hospitals that started as avowedly Jewish institutions clearly indicate their religious heritage. Mount Sinai is encountered eight times around the country. Two Jewish hospitals in Los Angeles have merged to form Cedars-Sinai Hospital, the "Cedars" being an abbreviation of Cedars of Lebanon. Other institutions bear the word "Jewish," "Hebrew," or "Beth Israel." In contrast, there are over 100 American hospitals named after St. Francis, almost 50 after St. Joseph and even 12 named Providence.

There is one Menorah Hospital and one Mount Zion Hospital. There are two Montefiores, one Maimonides, one Albert Einstein Center, a Jack Weiler Hospital and our own Miriam Hospital. A small number of hospitals, originally Jewish, now bear names that are more geographic in nature: Bronx-Lebanon in the Bronx and Kingsbrook in Brooklyn.

The imperatives of cost-containment and the realities of increasing competition for health care funds have led, inevitably, to the closing of some inefficient hospitals, and marketplace urgencies have overcome older ethnic allegiances, leading to all varieties of ecumenical mergers. In the last decade, half a dozen "mixed-marriages" have led to, for example, St. Francis-Mt. Sinai Medical Center in Hartford and Beth Israel-Deaconess Medical Center in Boston.

The historic imperatives which once created Jewish hospitals have largely disappeared. The great majority of American Jews is now native-born, no longer live in the inner cities and no longer need a health facility within walking distance. Jewish physicians are no longer restricted, by mindless prejudice, to hospitals of their own faith.

The many Jewish institutions which had once been sanctuaries for impoverished Jews are still supported by the Jewish community, but have now matured into great nonsectarian centers for clinical care, medical teaching and biomedical research.

In answer to the question: What makes a hospital Jewish? It becomes Jewish when it is blessed with an amalgamation of Jewish funding and some Jewish ambience, but mainly when it unilaterally declares itself to be Jewish.

The nurturing feminist from Henry Street

Germany in 1848 was in turmoil. Max Wahl, seeking a more stable way of life, migrated to the United States. He settled in the established and assimilated German-Jewish community of Cincinnati, changed his name to Wald, founded a secure optical business and married Minnie Schwarz. In time they had four children, one of whom was Lillian, born in March of 1867.

The gracious Wald home was, in the words of one family member, "more German than Jewish." The family, now quite prosperous, moved to Rochester, New York, to be closer

> *Columbia University asked Lillian Wald to help establish a degree-conferring program for nurses, one of the first in the world.*

to the wholesale optical industry. Lillian matured in an unthreatened, congenial, middle- class environment. Although the family maintained a membership in the Reform synagogue, it was secular affairs - English literature and classical music - which formed the dominate influences upon her life. A brief membership in the Ethical Culture movement constituted the sole evidence that Lillian sought spiritual guidance.

Lillian attended a privileged private school for young ladies, where students learned French, German, a bit of Latin, a smattering of astronomy and algebra, and those social graces needed to manage a proper household. At 15, Lillian applied to Vassar but was not admitted because of her relative youth. At 17, she rejected the notion of seeking a college education, which she disparagingly regarded as little more than a training program for marriage.

When Lillian's older sister, Julia, had difficulties during a pregnancy, a nurse was assigned to the home. And the nursing procedures that Lillian observed appealed to her deeply. Nursing, in 1890, was a relatively new profession. There were few graduate nurses, and most who provided nursing care were untrained and ill-prepared for their duties. The first professionalization of nursing was in England at St. Thomas' Hospital, some three decades before, under the stern direction of Florence Nightingale. In the United States, the first school of nursing was established at Bellevue Hospital, New York, in 1873. Lillian saw nursing as the answer to her desire for an occupation which would allow her some creative autonomy in a nurturing atmosphere. She entered New York Hospital School of Nursing in 1889.

Two years later, following her graduation, she elected to stay in Manhattan rather than return to Rochester. And with two colleagues from nursing school, she established a home, within the tenements, to aid the enormous numbers of immigrant Jews who were flooding into New York from the ghettos and villages of Eastern Europe.

In contrast to the German Jews who had arrived decades before and who strove to make themselves indistinguishable from the mainstream Protestants of the country, these newly-arrived Jews were ill-equipped to prosper in the urban sprawl of New York. They had to be trained, particularly the young immigrant mothers, in such rudimentary activities as the planning of nutritionally-balanced meals, shopping with currency, laundering, establishing budgets so that rents might be paid and above all, learning the English language.

Lillian and her two friends - her sisters in nursing - envisaged a house where education counseling and efficient nursing care might be rendered with only a minimum of payment, a place where the new arrivals might learn how to settle into the stressful living patterns of the Lower East Side. They called their modest establishment a settlement house. She also appreciated the extent to which home nursing (she called it public health nursing), through preventive interventions, might keep families together and raise the general level of health within the impoverished populations of the Manhattan ghettoes. Accordingly, she began the practice of home visits, particularly for the care of newborns and ailing mothers. She called her agency the Visiting Nurse Service.

Within two years her novel approach to community nursing and immigrant education caught the attention of the wealthy banker, Jacob Schiff, who then purchased a few buildings on Henry Street to house both components of Wald's enterprise. And within two decades the Henry Street Settlement House became a model of comprehensive care for an indigent population with meager resources. Nurses from all over the world came to be trained in Wald's establishment, and by 1914 the Settlement House had over 100 nurses employed to visit the neighborhood poor. Classes were conducted day and night to accommodate the compelling needs not only of the mothers but now, too, of the husbands seeking to integrate themselves into the way in which Americans lived and worked.

Columbia University asked Wald to help establish a degree-conferring program for nurses, one of the first in the world. Wald's concept of bringing the nurses to where they were needed led, inevitably, to the creation of the first public nursing program in the nation, in 1900. Wald's insistence also led to the development of a department for special education in New York City devoted to the unique needs, both medical and educational, of handicapped children.

Over the next few decades Wald became a leading advocate of women's rights (including the right to vote), the rights of labor unions to protect the health of workers, the right of minority members of the community to receive equal medical and nursing care (she was one of the founders of NAACP), the defense of Sacco and Vanzetti and the growing transnational pacifist movement.

After World War 1, Wald was instrumental in forming the Federal Children's Bureau in Washington. She numbered amongst her very close friends and supporters Sarah Roosevelt, mother of FDR.

Lillian Wald died in 1940 at age 73. She never married, rarely vacationed and except for the last few years of her life, lived where she worked in the wretched tenements of the Lower East Side of Manhattan. Generations of socially-oriented nurses and social workers have identified her as the mother of public health nursing, the one who conceived, assembled and ably managed the first settlement house and their sister in the splendid profession of human nursing. This German-Jewish woman eventually returned to her spiritual roots when the Jews of Germany were cruelly beset and she then recognized the need to identify openly with her coreligionists. Yet, in truth, her entire professional life had been in the service of deprived Jews.

In recent years the U.S. Postal Service has created a postage stamp to honor her memory.

Goldwater and the evolution
of the modern hospital

Sigismund Shulz Goldwater, M.D., a New York physician born over 125 years ago, did much to shape the physical character and professional purpose of 20th-century hospitals here and abroad. But to understand the expanding agenda of the modern hospital, to understand the forces which critically transformed the institution over the centuries, and to appreciate Dr. Goldwater's seminal role in this maturation, the changing purposes which society has assigned to hospitals must first be explored.

The present-day hospital fulfills many interdependent functions: as a community resource for emergency therapies; as an inpatient center for the skilled employment of sophisticated diagnostic and life-saving technologies; as a learning center employing physicians, nurses and allied health technicians; as an outreach program providing care — particularly maternal and pediatric care — for a needy ambulatory community; as a center for the diagnosis and treatment of such socially oriented ills as chemical dependencies, and, increasingly, as a place to conduct dedicated biomedical and clinical research.

Clearly, the modern hospital is a complex and expensive enterprise, consuming many resources, touching more lives and saving more lives than ever before. But to the individual patient, often intimidated by the immensity and impersonal nature of the medical center, the modern hospital is more formidable than hospitable. And with few exceptions, it is no longer a familiar, and cherished, community facility.

In contrast, the typical western European hospital at the beginning of the second millennium, in the year 1000, was a rudimentary retreat, more theological in purpose than medical. It was primarily in the business of providing custodial rather than curative care. Indeed, its name is etymologically related to such words as hospice and hotel, betraying its original function as a shelter. Hospitality, to this day, describes congeniality, warmth and neighborliness.

The hospitals of medieval England, before the Norman invasion nine centuries ago, were few in number and without regulatory standards. Their guiding purpose, however, was unambiguous: they were established for the salvation of souls, and only incidentally for the alleviation of pain and disability. It was widely accepted that physical disease was the legacy of sin, and if illness was a divine punishment, then cure could only be achieved by nullifying the sinful realities that prompted the punishment. And this was church business. In short, 11th-century physicians had little to do with hospitals.

By the 13th century, hospitals were serving a broader function: as an infirmary for the sick, as a hostel for weary travelers, as a haven for the blind, as an asylum for the mad, as a hospice for the dying, as a hotel for the indigent pilgrim and wandering cleric, and particularly as a leprosarium. The dramatic rise of leprosy and other pestilences gave impetus to a more formal medical role in the historic affairs of the hospital.

The medieval hospital was usually built at the outer gates of the city, at holy sites (typically, springs called holy wells) or at river crossings. They were managed by religious or military orders (such as the Knights Templar). Their architectural design was simple. Food and wood for heating were obtained from adjacent farmlands and forest. Additional maintenance funds came from bequests and alms. The patient was given clothing, shelter, warmth and food; in turn, he was expected to participate in all prayers, endure his infirmity with equanimity, fulfill chores assigned to him, work in the fields, be obedient and maintain chastity.

The outlines of the 19th-century American hospitals can best be seen in the unfolding growth of the London hospitals of the late Middle Ages. One of the first great institutions was established in 1122 at a Thames crossing as an Augustinian priory. It named its small infirmary after St. Thomas and for four centuries it served a crowded London through plagues, civil wars and great fires. Henry VIII appropriated all of its funds in 1540 (remember, it was a church-run institution) which led, eventually, to a secularization of its administration and a freedom to grow. Business leaders then managed the institution, assuming a parental role and overseeing a rudimentary medical welfare system. The hospital remained a haven solely for poor people.

By the 19th century, St. Thomas had grown into a huge institution with its own medical school. In 1860 a remarkable woman, Florence

Nightingale by name, started a nursing school at St. Thomas, the first in the Western world. Nursing required a hospital setting to become a profession parallel to medicine.

Yet another great institution had its rude beginnings in the 12th century as a primitive shelter dedicated to the apostle St. Bartholomew. This hospital, in the center of London and called Bart's, fulfilled a curious role in a city without a central police department. Bart's had its own policemen (called beadles) who roamed the streets picking up the dying, the lepers, the inebriated, and the dissolute. The goal of the hospital was not salvation as much as moral rectitude, and as a means of protecting the established community Bart's became a huge disease-oriented prison.

And for the mentally deranged, there was an institution called St. Mary's of Bethlehem (pronounced Bedlam) founded in the year 1247. It was a place of horror and administrative corruption giving newer meaning to the word bedlam. It had been jointly administered with Bridewell, the prison for vagrants and debtors. But this too changed and Bethlehem evolved into a more compassionate institution, finally changing its name to the Institute of Psychiatry, world famous as a site for research and the training of mental health workers.

The English hospitals thus began as a shelter for the pilgrim and a place for the salvation of the soul; then a site to quarantine the contagious ones in order to protect the greater community; then a paternalistic welfare facility for the impoverished; then, and still, a place for the poor and chronically ill.

The hospitals of the United States, during the 18th and 19th centuries were no more efficient or compassionate than their English counterparts. They followed a similar pattern of growth in function and purpose.

A young New Yorker named Sigismund Goldwater received his M.D. degree from the medical school at New York University-Bellevue at the dawn of the 20th century and vowed to change the function, the population served and even the architecture of the hospitals of the new century.

Goldwater: America's pioneer hospital administrator

Mount Sinai Hospital (initially called The Jews' Hospital) was founded on Feb. 16, 1851 when the Hebrew Benevolent Society voted to assign $1,034.16 to begin its construction on West 28th Street in Manhattan. An unsolicited gift of $20,000 from Judah Touro* allowed the planners to design a princely institution of 45 beds. It was unique in that it boasted gas illumination and sources of running water on all four of its spacious floors. It was the city's third private hospital (preceded by New York Hospital and St. Vincent's Hospital), and from its initial years it was resolutely non-sectarian. Many of its leading physicians, including Valentine Mott and Willard Parker, were not Jews.

During the Civil War, and particularly following the tragic draft riots of 1863, the U.S. Army commandeered the hospital for the care of its wartime casualties. A new Mt. Sinai Hospital, of 69 beds, was then constructed on East 67th Street. By 19th-century standards, it was an elegant, spacious and well-ventilated establishment and one of the first hospitals to accept women for internships.

One of the interns was a young New Yorker named Sigismund Shulz Goldwater, the son of a middle-class German-Jewish family. Sigismund (called by family and friends, "SS") attended Columbia University, but then took a leave of absence to enroll in Leipzig University for further studies in philosophy. It was during his *wanderjahr* in the Carpathians that SS decided upon a career in medicine and specifically public health medicine. Following his return to New York, he enrolled in New York University's College of Medicine and was awarded his M.D. degree in 1900.

Shortly after beginning his graduate training at Mt. Sinai, SS approached the chairman of its board, George Blumenthal, with an unusual request: to foreswear clinical medicine and train instead for an administrative position eventually to manage the hospital. Something about Goldwater's assertiveness and vision appealed to Blumenthal. He sent the young physician to Europe for a year of study in the continent's great hospitals. In 1902 at age 29, Goldwater returned to assume the daily management of Mt. Sinai Hospital.

This was a critical juncture in the history of the institution. Because it was rapidly outgrowing its facilities on 67th Street, funds were sought for a new hospital to be constructed further north, adjacent to Central Park at 100th Street and Fifth Avenue. Goldwater's radical vision created a boldly designed medical center which included his revolutionary idea that a private pavilion be established with funding eventually from the Guggenheim family. Until then, hospitals had operated essentially for the poor and dispossessed. The established classes had their babies delivered at home and rarely used hospitals except for major surgery. Minor surgery, by custom, was undertaken in the private physician's office.

The new Mt. Sinai also included a separate pediatric pavilion with balconies and solaria on each floor and roof gardens for ambulatory children. Goldwater had classrooms built adjacent to the wards since many of the children were hospitalized for extended intervals. In 1906 Mt. Sinai became the fourth hospital in the country to create a separate social service department. The Lewisohn family contributed funds so that a separate laboratory and research pavilion might be built where, amongst other significant discoveries, the feasibility of blood transfusions was first determined.

Goldwater's medical background ensured that the latest diagnostic and therapeutic instruments were available, including one of the first X-ray departments in the country. For that he faced a problem: no available space. Rather than wait until a new wing could be constructed, Goldwater had the X-ray unit installed in the rear of the hospital's synagogue. Yet he was not insensitive to the spiritual needs of his coreligionists. The kitchens were kosher and the hospital maintained a staff of Yiddish-English translators.

During the next decade, Goldwater established an exemplary outpatient service, with 200,000 visits per year, the largest in the city. He also created satellite clinics in poorer neighborhoods within the referral region of the hospital. As the fame and reputation of the hospital grew, the U.S. Army asked Mt. Sinai to recruit and manage an army hospital (which, during World War I, served with distinction in Bordeaux, France, and in World War II, in Africa, Italy and France).

Goldwater's genius for innovative uses of clinics and his skills as a hospital administrator culminated in his appointment in 1914 as New York's Commissioner of Health. As commissioner, he established the city's program in compulsory vaccination for all children and a Bureau of Industrial Hygiene.

During the next two decades, Goldwater's aptitudes in planning hospitals flourished. He designed both the buildings and the tables of administrative organization for over 250 hospitals in the United States and abroad, including the American Hospital in Paris, St. Paul's Hospital in Manila, Leningrad's University Hospital and Tokyo's St. Luke's Hospital.

While working as consultant to innumerable cities, Goldwater maintained his attachment to Mt. Sinai Hospital. In the 1930s, for example, he was instrumental in having the hospital recruit (and retrain when necessary) 182 physicians, all refugees from Nazi Germany.

Mayor LaGuardia of New York, confronted with an aging and corrupt municipal hospital system, appointed Goldwater to reorganize and rebuild it. These hospitals, including such venerable institutions as Kings County and Bellevue Hospitals, were rebuilt, restaffed, and many converted to teaching institutions affiliated with medical schools. And when the city completed a new municipal hospital for chronic disease on Welfare Island, it was only natural that it be called Goldwater Hospital.

Goldwater's final position was as president of a newly established health insurance organization called Blue Cross. He died in 1950.

Goldwater provided inspired guidance to a generation of hospital architects and administrators. He helped to convert the drab city hospitals, cruel warehouses for the poor, into humane institutions, places for rehabilitation, education and hope.

Editor's Note: Judah Touro was a son of the first spiritual leader of the synagogue in Newport, which in later years bore the family name because the street running in front of the *shul* was named for Judah and his brother, each of whom made bequests to the City of Newport, one to keep the street paved and another to help pay a rabbi. Judah Touro left the northeast in the early 1800s and established trading businesses in New Orleans, where he also funded a nonsectarian hospital that bears his name.

Dr. Hannah Stone, the madonna of the clinic

The year was 1916. A courageous and determined nurse named Margaret Higgins Sanger searched tirelessly for a site to establish a facility where uneducated mothers might be taught that birth control rather than illegal abortion was the more rational approach to family planning.

The Comstock Laws of 1873 made illegal the manufacture, sale or distribution of contraceptive devices, and the advocacy of, or instruction in, family planning procedures either directly or via the postal system, was similarly a punishable offense. Sanger therefore sought a neighborhood where such a clinic was desperately needed and a community where, despite its illegal nature, family planning instruction would be congenially received. She chose the predominantly Jewish neighborhood of Brownsville in Brooklyn to establish, in October of 1916, the first birth-control clinic in the United States.

After renting a two-room apartment in a tenement at 46 Amboy St., just off Pitkin Avenue, she distributed handbills in Yiddish, English and Italian, saying: "Mothers: Can you afford to have a large family ? Do you want any more children? If not, why do you have them? Do not kill. Do not take life, but prevent. Safe, harmless information can be obtained from trained nurses. Tell your neighbors and friends. All mothers welcome. A registration fee of ten cents entitles any mother to this information."

The clinic was besieged by women. On its first day of operation, 140 women were counseled. Within 12 days, though, the police raided the facility, destroyed the records and arrested Sanger and her colleagues on charges of obscenity. The destruction of the clinic and the imprisonment of its personnel convinced Sanger that a viable clinic dispensing birth-control paraphernalia could be sustained only if the Comstock Laws were abolished; or, alternatively, if government intervention were shown to subvert the sanctity of the patient-physician relationship. Overturning these antediluvian laws, in 1916, seemed to be too daunting a task. Similarly, proving in court that these laws invaded the privacy of the physician's consultation room could not be accomplished unless a physician was actively involved. Accordingly, Sanger's next task was to recruit a licensed physician. This proved to be no easy matter since many of the New York hospitals were opposed to any form of birth control and would remove the staff privileges of any doctor knowingly engaged in birth-control medicine.

Sanger's answer came in the form of a diminutive Jewish physician from Brooklyn. Her name was Hannah Mayer Stone, M.D. She was born in New York in 1893, the daughter of educated parents (her father was the neighborhood pharmacist). Hannah studied pharmacy at Brooklyn College. In 1912, she was employed by Bellevue Hospital as a bacteriologist; and there she met Abraham Stone, a young medical intern. They married and while her new husband was in the army, Hannah herself attended medical school, receiving her M.D. degree in 1920. The couple then established a joint practice in Manhattan.

Dr. Stone first heard Margaret Sanger in 1921 during the plenary sessions of the first American Birth Control Conference. Indeed, she witnessed Sanger being arrested in Town Hall when delivering a speech advocating birth control. An outraged Dr. Stone then joined the advisory board of the clinic and in 1923 accepted Sanger's invitation to manage, without salary, a private family planning clinic in lower Manhattan.

From then until her untimely death in 1941, Dr. Stone directed this clinic with dedication. Sanger later wrote, "Her gaze was clear and straight, her hair was black, her mouth gentle and sweet. She had a sympathetic response to mothers in distress and a broad attitude towards life's many problems. She came to be known as the madonna of the clinic."

Dr. Stone did not keep a diary so it is not known whether she was bemused by this non-Jewish sobriquet.

Because Dr. Stone maintained careful records on over 100,000 patients, she was able to determine the degree of success of various birth-control modalities. In the course of her 18 years as the director of the clinic, she devised a number of successful contraceptive chemicals, devices and procedures. Her many articles, textbooks and lectures educated a generation of physicians in marital counseling and family planning. In 1936 the American Medical Association declared family planning to be a necessary component of the practice of medicine.

During the next decade Dr. Stone was repeatedly harassed by police interventions and on one occasion was arrested on charges of indecency (as defined in Section 1142 of the Penal Code, which declared that the dissemination of contraceptive information was a form of pornography). The National Council of Jewish Women then expressed their support for Dr. Stone and officially endorsed birth control as a worthy undertaking.

In 1931, the Central Conference of American Rabbis as well as central bodies representing the Presbyterian, Methodist and Congregationalist faiths also advocated family planning clinics. They affirmed that morality should be based upon knowledge and freedom, not ignorance.

In 1936, Dr. Stone ordered a box of medical pessaries from Japan. She then informed the U.S. Customs Service of its imminent arrival. The package was promptly seized and Dr. Stone then sued the government to recover the package, based upon her contention that a licensed physician may freely import medical equipment for legitimate therapies designed to protect or enhance the health of the patient. In December of 1936 the federal Circuit Court of Appeals of the Second Circuit Court ruled in her favor. Morris Ernst, one of her lawyers, commented: "Nowhere in its opinion did the court specifically state under what circumstances a doctor was free to prescribe a contraceptive. The inference was clear that the medical profession was to be the sole judge of the propriety of prescription in a given case, and that as long as a physician exercised his discretion in good faith, the legality of his action was not to be questioned."

In 1941, at age 48, Hannah Stone died of a heart attack. At memorial services, Sanger declared: "Thousands of mothers owed their peace of mind, marital harmony, health, and yes, in many instances, life itself, to Hannah Stone." Her work was continued by her husband Abraham. During the decades that the Stones managed this country's first and foremost birth control clinic, thousands of young medical students (including the author of this column) climbed the steps of the Manhattan brownstone to learn the rudiments of marital counseling and the importance of giving to those who bear children the right to freely choose each pregnancy.

Chapter 4

Simon Baruch, father of Lower East Side bathhouses

The son of Neriah and trusted friend of Jeremiah the prophet was called Baruch (Jeremiah 32:12). Three others, mentioned in various books of the Bible, also carry this exalted name, meaning blessed. As a family name, Baruch was chosen by some Jews living in medieval Germany.

Simon Baruch, born in 1840, left his native Prussia to escape imminent military conscription, and at age 15 he voyaged alone to these shores. He knew only one distant relative in America, a Mannes Baum who owned a general store in Camden, South Carolina. For the next few years, young Simon learned English while working as the store's bookkeeper. The Baums, convinced of Simon's native intellectual abilities, sent him to South Carolina Medical College in Charleston. He later transferred to the Medical College of Virginia where, in 1862, he was awarded the M.D. degree. Dr. Baruch joined the armies of the Confederacy, was senior surgeon to a South Carolina infantry division, was twice captured by the Union Army, and at the end of the Civil War had returned to South Carolina, where he helped to establish the state Medical Society and was appointed as president of the state's Board of Health.

Dr. Baruch practiced medicine in South Carolina for the succeeding 16 years but was increasingly dissatisfied with the indiscriminate use of unproven remedies which, as often as not, did more visible harm than good. His studies brought him to appreciate the healing philosophies of Vincent Priessnitz (1799-1852), who had established a hugely successful therapeutic spa at Grafenberg in the Austrian Silesia. Priessnitz used therapies confined to the use of cold water for frequent bathing and for irrigating the gastro-intestinal tract. He confined his patients to a mountainside retreat, allowing them a modest diet, no tobacco or alcohol, and much exercise in a tranquil, stress-free atmosphere. He called this alternate form of medicine hydropathy (or hydrotherapy).

Dr. Baruch found little in the realm of the conventional therapies of the 1870s to meet his definition of appropriate medical care. With the exception of proven medications such as digitalis leaf, morphine and a few others, he was certain that the vast bulk of untested and unregulated chemicals and herbal extracts created more harm than benefit. His advocacy of minimal medical intervention came close to the views of William Osler and others who recommended doing nothing rather than doing harm, a phase of medical history sometimes called nihilism.

South Carolina offered him no further challenges and he elected to move his practice and his family to New York City.

His defense of hydrotherapy found critics in New York; but there were many who flocked to his office for a treatment regime that avoided the standard drugs of the day which included the many mercurial and arsenical pharmaceuticals, the herbal decoctions, the mindless use of purgatives and opiates as well as the discredited bleedings.

Hydrotherapy found a willing audience since medicine in the late 19th century had little specific to offer. It would be decades before proven anti-syphilitic agents became available as well as newer drugs to combat heart failure and aid the kidneys in excreting burdensome body fluids. Rational therapies for glandular diseases and diabetes would not appear for many years.

Dr. Baruch now confronted something that he had not previously encountered in the cities of South Carolina. He saw the great masses of newly arrived Jewish immigrants living in the congested tenements of the Lower East Side of the island of Manhattan. Laws had not yet been passed to standardize the hygienic facilities of these crowded warrens. Apartments consisted of little more than airless bedrooms and perhaps a kitchen but no private bathrooms. The older structures had outhouses behind the tenement, while some of the newer tenements had indoor privies, one for each cluster of four or more apartments, but neither baths nor showers.

Over a century of memory lapses and fond mythologies have softened the image of tenement life in the New York City of 1880. The quaint tales of thriving Jewish life, of enterprising young people advancing from the pushcart to the little general store to the massive department store, of families overcoming poverty, have somehow ignored the tragically high infant mortality rate, the many broken homes and the life expectancies which rarely exceeded 40 years.

Dr. Baruch witnessed how many fellow Jews were left behind in the slow progress toward middle-class self sufficiency. He noted the rampant enteric infections and tuberculosis within this embattled community, the utter absence of sanitary facilities and the unavoidable squalor. "The great unwashed" was a description born of stark reality. His social conscience now combined with his faith in hydrotherapy to launch a campaign that would immortalize his name amongst the impoverished immigrants of the Lower East Side.

Using funds gathered from his successful practice of medicine, Dr. Baruch proceeded to construct a series of public baths throughout the neighborhood. These imposing buildings — a few still standing as remembrances of what had once been — provided a place for the poor to bathe at frequent intervals, and these free facilities, conjoined with a community-based educational effort to inculcate the principles of basic personal hygiene amongst the newly arrived Jews, changed the morbidity and mortality rates dramatically. The health of the immigrant Jewish community improved immensely with the arrival of socially conscious organizations such as the Henry Street Settlement House.

Despite persuasive advocates such as Lust, Baruch and Kellogg (of corn flakes fame), hydrotherapy faded as a significant school of therapy. The Baruch bathhouses endured until the second decade of the 20th century, when the laws of New York City required private bathrooms in all apartment houses.

And Dr. Baruch, the apostle of cleanliness? He lived to see his children grow to maturity, including the great Bernard Baruch, financial advisor to six presidents of the United States.

His gift of public bathhouses seems modest by current standards. But to a generation of unlettered, unwashed immigrants it was a salvation which taught the lessons of cleanliness, dignity and generosity. And when, some years ago, New York City built a shiny new junior high school on East 21st Street, they named it the Simon Baruch Middle School in remembrance of a German-Jewish refugee of blessed memory.

A neglected commandment: 'Honor thy father and thy mother'

I ts words are part of a sacred Decalogue, widely and reverently quoted; and though this solemn declaration is visibly enshrined on countless walls, it sometimes goes unheeded: "Honor thy father and thy mother." (Exodus 20: 12).

The withholding of honor that should have been accorded to parents (and, by inference, to all elderly persons) may take many forms, ranging from mild indifference to neglect to exploitation or, at worst, even physical abuse and abandonment. Until recently, this shameful act had no name; but in its most flagrant form we now call it elder abuse, a phrase whispered rather than shouted, since its very existence bespeaks of a profound moral lapse in responsibility.

How common is elder abuse? It is a crime that is neither readily nor easily documented; nor is it a subject that arises spontaneously or willingly in conversations at social gatherings. Some will even deny its existence, saying that elder abuse is unknown in their neighborhood while admitting, begrudgingly, that it may possibly be found in other communities. Police and social scientists, on the other hand, will readily verify its existence in all cultures and ethnic groups.

According to available statistics, and probably representing a substantial under-reporting, about one person in 10 older than 65 years is the victim of some form of elder abuse every year. Translating this to the Rhode Island community, it would mean that there are about 7,500 instances of reportable elder abuse in this state annually, and in about 3,000 of these instances, the abuse is sufficiently grave to require medical intervention or an emergency room visit.

Most instances of elder abuse, perhaps the great majority, go unreported by the victim for a variety of compelling reasons: fear of not being believed; fear of being "put away," institutionalized; fear of retaliation by the abuser; fear of being ostracized by the remaining members of the family. And, of course, many elderly, particularly those who are confused, do not understand either the dynamics or the extent to which they are abused, and they may avoid asking for help because they conclude that they are in some way personally to blame for their abuse.

Elder abuse did not suddenly start when the amendments to the Older Americans Act were approved by Congress in 1987. It has been part of communal life for millennia; and it must have been a visible element in the lives of ancient communities for its prohibition to have been cited repeatedly in the Torah. Elder abuse may be personal, carried out by someone known to the elder person, usually a close member of the family; or elder abuse may be institutional, a nursing home, perhaps, with the fiduciary responsibility for the continuing care of the elder person. In less common circumstances, it may be a pathological self-neglect, the behavior of an elderly person indifferent to his or her welfare or safety.

Elder abuse may assume many forms:

1. **Physical abuse**: Defined as the use of physical force causing bodily injury, physical pain or actions leading to impairment of function. This may include acts of violence (pushing, beating, shaking, slapping) but physical abuse also includes the inappropriate use of physical restraints or medications (particularly sedative agents).

2. **Sexual abuse:** Defined as non-consensual sexual contact of any kind with an elderly individual. This category includes unwanted touching.

3. **Emotional abuse**: Through verbal or nonverbal means, the infliction of distress, anxiety, anguish, pain or fear upon an elderly person. This form of abuse, perhaps the most commonly practiced type of abuse and certainly the most difficult to verify, includes intimidation, humiliation, harassment, infantilization or isolating the elderly person; and in its most subtle form, treating the vulnerable elderly as though they were incapable of intelligent conversation. They have been rendered invisible in the eyes of the abuser.

4. **Neglect**: Defined as the failure to fulfill a person's (or an institution's) fiduciary responsibility for the care and welfare of the elderly person. Specifically, it includes neglect of such essentials as water, food, clothing, shelter, adequate hygiene, prescribed medications, and such measures as are needed for the physical safety of the elder person.

5. **Financial exploitation**: Defined as the illegal use of an elder's financial resources, property or other tangible assets. The forging of an elder's signature is considered a part of this category.

6. **Abandonment**: Defined as the willful desertion of an elderly individual by a person or institution bearing the continuing responsibility of that elderly person.

Who are the abusers? The overwhelming majority are family members (spouse, child, etc.) serving as the designated caregivers.

Physicians may sometimes be the first to suspect the existence of elder abuse when encountering an elderly patient in the home with inappropriate *cachexia* (a generally weakened, emaciated condition of the body), poor personal hygiene, excessive anxieties and evidence of bruises.

Institutional abuse is to be considered when such complications as repeated bed sores are encountered.

On the day that this column was being assembled, the *Providence Journal* carried a front-page story with the headline, "National report finds abuse rising in nursing homes." The story went on to give details of a Congressional investigation which noted that nearly one-third of all registered nursing homes, some 5,283 of a national total of about 17,000, had been cited for elder-abuse violations in the past two years. It should be remembered that about 1.5 million Americans are long-term residents of nursing homes.

Is it possible; is it even conceivable, that an elderly Jewish person might be abused by a close relative in this day and age? A moment's reflection tells us that elder abuse can also be a subtle event that leaves neither visible bruises nor fractured bones; it might be an impatience or the treating of grandma who has a memory problem as though she were an infant rather than a person deserving of compassion.

And have elderly Jews sometimes been abused, neglected, and even abandoned in millennia past? Psalm 71 carries these words: "Cast me not off in the time of old age; forsake me not when my strength fails." And in more recent years, read those anguished letters published in the *Bintel Briefs* (Bundle of Letters) section of *The Jewish Daily Forward*. It was rare, admittedly; but it was there in the 1920s and '30s. And today?

But the Lord looketh in the heart

There is hardly a human organ which, at some time in history, has not served as a metaphor for some human attribute. The liver, for example, once thought of as the seat of human strength and spirit, has yielded such meaningful expressions as "lily-livered" and "yellow-livered." But the heart, more than any other organ, has been chosen to symbolize an astonishing range of human characteristics and behaviors.

Most organs sit quietly within the body cavities performing their physiological functions without any visible display; and the duties assigned to them by our primitive ancestors therefore tended to represent fanciful speculation rather than rational study. The heart, in contrast to other organs, regularly moved, throbbed, even palpitated. Surely, thought the ancients, this organ must be the core monitor of the body managing the other, subsidiary organs while also initiating one's thinking and determining one's personal destiny.

Aristotle, noting that the heart rate accelerated in times of stress, anxiety or passion, concluded that the heart must certainly control the body including its capacity to remember and think. The nomadic Hebrews had similar views. And the Hebrew Bible therefore contains numerous phrases with allusions to the heart as the representation of many human virtues and faculties.

The heart was said to be the seat of happiness ("wine that cheers the hearts of men," Psalms 104:15); it was the place where refractory behavior originates ("And Pharaoh's heart was hardened, and he hearkened not unto them." "And the Lord said unto Moses, Pharaoh's heart is stubborn, he refuseth to let the people go," Exodus 7:13-14; 8:15; 9:35); the seat of trembling and anxiety ("The Lord shall give you there an anguished heart," Deut. 28:63); the site of grief and dismay ("His heart was saddened," Deut. 6:6); locus of total moral commitment ("...love the Lord with all your heart and soul," Deut. 13:4); the authentic character of a person ("As he thinketh in his heart, so is he," Proverbs 23:7); the site of true atonement ("A broken and contrite heart," Psalms 51:17); an awareness of the fundamental sadness of life ("Even in laughter the heart is sorrowful." Proverbs 14:13); The source of ungoverned emotions ("For the imagination of man's heart is evil from his youth," Genesis 8:21); the source of life-fulfilling joy ("Gladness of the heart is the life of a man, and the joyfulness of a man prolongeth his days," Ecclesiasticus 30:22); and where faith in one's personal judgment can be found ("Let the counsel of thine own heart stand," Ecclesiasticus 37:13).

But with all these cardiac allusions in the Scriptures, are there any events within its many books that hint of heart disease? Specifically, is there anything in the Bible to suggest the existence of coronary disease, angina, heart failure or any other manifestations of cardiac impairment amongst the ancient Hebrews?*

There are no Biblical passages that convincingly depict heart disease. But why should there be, one might ask, since the Bible was never intended to serve as a clinical text? Yet in its candid portrayal of mankind, the Bible describes unsavory human behavior including rape, murder, adultery, incest, idolatry and interpersonal betrayal; and it provides, in passing, adequate descriptions of stroke, epilepsy, leprosy, mental disease and various skin disorders. Then why not heart disease?

Heart disease (the major cause of morbidity and mortality in the Western world), is singularly unmentioned in the Bible. Some may point to the story of Jacob's anguish (Genesis 45:25-26), claiming that this may represent an instance of a heart attack brought on by acute distress. ("They went up from Egypt and came to their father Jacob in the land of Canaan. And they told him, 'Joseph is still alive; yes, he is ruler over the whole land of Egypt.' Jacob's heart went numb, for he did not believe them.") More likely when citing the numbness of Jacob's heart the authors of Genesis were exercising permissible poetic license in portraying his emotional shock.

But if the Bible lacks a credible description of cardiovascular disease (perhaps because heart disease was indeed rare in ancient times) it does nonetheless contain a brief episode which indicates the remote possibility that the Scriptural authors had some dim understanding of the role of diet in the causation of human disease, and perhaps cardiovascular disease.

The Book of Daniel relates the story of the military defeat of Judah by the Babylonian King Nebuchadnezzar. The Babylonians then kidnapped four Israelite youths of royal heritage (Daniel, Hananiah,

Mishael, and Azariah) to train them in the Chaldean language, religion and customs so that they may eventually serve in the royal palace. Furthermore, the king allotted to them special rations of meat and wine from his royal kitchens.

Daniel, one of the four Israelite youths, resolved not to defile himself by eating the king's non-kosher food; and accordingly he requested permission to abstain. The jailer responded by saying that any other diet might make the captured youths look pale and undernourished. Daniel replied: "Please test us for 10 days, giving us pulses (legumes) to eat and water to drink. Then compare our appearance with that of the youths who eat the king's food, and do with us as you see fit." And when the 10 days were over, they looked better and healthier than all the youths who had been eating of the king's food and wine. When the time came to present the captured youths to King Nebuchadnezzar, the four who were maintained on a diet restricted to legumes appeared the healthiest and even the wisest and most proficient in languages.

The Book of Daniel declares that the superiority of the four Israelite youths came about because of the Lord's intervention in their behalf. But if the reference to a leguminous diet was not merely a casual bit of narrative, then it is not beyond the realm of exegetical inquiry to presume that this high-protein vegetarian diet was also a health-promoting factor. Someone may have observed, then, that a diet heavy in meat and wine, when compared with a lean vegetarian diet, was associated with a higher frequency of life-shortening disease; and, thinking this important, incorporated it in the Book of Daniel.

As modern Bible scholarship has pointed out, the ancient writers and editors of the Hebrew Bible perceived the heart primarily as the seat of the intellect and the emotions. The Bible routinely uses the Hebrew word *lev*, "heart," when describing what we now regard as responses of the mind or brain. This may explain the Bible's failure to refer to heart disease as a physical phenomenon.

What makes a proverb Yiddish?

My cupping runneth over

A proverb is a saying, an aphorism or an admonition concerning some commonplace human activity expressed in a succinct, frequently memorable phrase. It is often an allegoric distillation of some moral truth firmly embedded in the ethos of the local culture. In family terms, proverbs are Grandma's kitchen sayings refined and elaborated on by decades of telling and retelling.

Jewish folklore is sprinkled with adages, maxims and proverbs, some with an uncomplimentary medical coloring. For example, *"Der doktor hot a refueh tsu alts, oder nit tzu dales."* (The doctor has a remedy for everything but poverty.) Or, *"A doktor un a kvors man zeinen shutfim."* (Doctors and gravediggers are partners.) Here's another proverb to describe medical treatments, *"Oder es helft nit oder men darf es nit."* (Either it doesn't help or it's not needed.) Finally, the ultimate Yiddish proverb, *"Altsding lszt zich ois mit a gevein."* (Everything ends in weeping.)

One of the most memorable of Yiddish adages is, *"Es vet helfen vi oyf toyten bankes."* (It will help as readily as a cupping will revive a dead person.)

Contrary to some persistent views, cupping was not invented to punish children living in the ghettos of Manhattan's Lower East Side during the early years of the 20th century. Cupping actually represents a crucial therapeutic modality in classical Chinese medicine, was adopted by practitioners of Arabic medicine a millennium ago and still persists today in many parts of Asia.

The original procedure consisted of heating the air within segments of hollow bamboo reeds and placing the open end of the cuplike bamboo onto the skin of the chest, back or buttocks.

Later practitioners substituted ornamented glass cups so that they might observe the change in the skin being cupped. Heating the interior of the cup removed the oxygen, so that when the cup was applied vigorously to the skin, the air within cooled, thus suctioning up the subjacent skin while maintaining a tight bond between cup and skin.

The residual heat caused the covered skin to redden, often with a first-degree burn.

Cupping was prescribed for patients with chest inflammation, asthma, or congestion in the mistaken notion that the intentional inflammation of the skin would draw away the inflammation in the deeper organs. It was also used for chronic arthritis and a number of other ill-defined conditions. Cupping was sometimes performed on areas of skin that had been intentionally lacerated; and thus when the heated cups were applied, blood oozed from the cuts in a method akin to blood-letting. An alternative therapy consisted of placing a burning piece of wood or herb upon the skin, an intervention called *moxibustion* (from a Japanese word, *moxa,* meaning burning herb).

The time is 1925. Somewhere in the Jewish tenements of the Lower East Side a typical scenario unfolds: a child, perhaps five years of age, develops croup with fever and a nasty, resonant cough. The physician making a house call recommends cupping, and the mother or an older sibling then hastens to the local barbershop to summon a barber skilled in the art. (One easily recognizes which barbers perform cupping by seeing the cupping set prominently displayed in the front window.) The barber arrives at the apartment carrying his cupping satchel. He places a lighted tallow candle on a side table and then silently applies a thin layer of a lubricant oil over the child's chest and back. He carefully heats each cup over the candle flame and quickly presses it (with its interior air now exhausted by the flame) upon the child's skin and holds it there until it sucks up the underlying skin. A typical cupping episode consists of six cups applied to the chest; but when the fever is high, 12 cups are applied and it is then called double-cupping. The cups are removed after about an hour, leaving circular burn lines where the hot rim had been in contact with the skin. The reddened skin remains raised and tender for a day or more. The distinctive smell of burning skin lingers in the room for hours, and the wretched memories of the pain and terror last a lifetime.

Tribal memories of things pleasant or unpleasant persist in tales that grandmothers relate, in stories told around the dinner table, and even in pretentious proverbs.

Proverbs speak in generalizations; and generalizations are dangerous. The hazards in sweeping, pithy proverbs are, to coin a term, proverbial.

Indeed, any generalization serves to lessen the accuracy of the proverb since many such adages do not admit exceptions. Consider, for example, "When the cat's away, the mice will play." Perhaps sometimes; but on the other hand, when the cat is on sabbatical, the mice might also elect to sleep, eat or meditate upon their historically insecure existence, rather than play.

The value of a proverb as an educational instrument will therefore depend on its clarity and effectiveness as a metaphor rather than its role as a literal statement. "Don't put all your eggs in one basket," will not be understood by those who assign little value to eggs or tend to grasp their baskets firmly. Many, many proverbs then end their lives as sententious claptrap suitable only for embroidered samplers or uncritical Sunday school sermons.

Why then does an ancient proverb such as *"Svet helfn vi a toyten bankes,"* have such enduring merit, even for a modern population that would never dream of allowing cupping on its children? For one thing, the proverb has vivid imagery. Think of the utter absurdity of employing an antiquated and painful procedure such as cupping, on a moldering corpse. There is, in this scene, pathos wedded to irony and enhanced by typical Yiddish hyperbole. To paraphrase the proverb; "Whatever you are recommending is asinine, no, it is worse than asinine, it is preposterous. It has as much merit as this most therapeutically inept of interventions."

Finally, what makes a proverb Yiddish? When it is insightful, poignant yet humorous; when it resorts to far-fetched, implausible poetic equivalents that defy reason much like the floating figures in Marc Chagall's paintings defy gravity. And, of course, the so-called Yiddish proverbs should make you grin, shake your head and remark *"Git gezugt!"*

'You have trachoma, you cannot enter'

Trachoma was certainly present in the poor Jewish communities of Eastern Europe. But it was then regarded as merely one of many burdensome medical infirmities, such as tuberculosis, typhus and cholera. Trachoma assumed critical importance in Jewish thinking, however, only when the United States Immigration Service declared trachoma to be one of a number of physical and mental disabilities barring admission to these shores.

Informal medical inspections of arriving immigrants had been customary. But in 1892 an outbreak of cholera prompted President Benjamin Harrison to issue an order declaring the need to inspect all immigrants. This hastened the development of the U.S. Public Health Service to establish formal criteria listing those disorders, which would bar any immigrant from this nation.

Ellis Island in New York harbor became the principal gateway for immigrants seeking admission. Each immigrant went through an anxiety-generating examination in the great hall of the imposing red brick structure called by many "the Palace of Tears." A public health physician scrutinized each person and chalk marks were then affixed to their clothing. For example, a letter "G" signified goiter, a letter "X" for apparent mental illness, a letter "L" for lameness and a letter "T" for trachoma. The eyelids of each immigrant were everted and any severe inflammation was interpreted as evidence of trachoma and therefore grounds for returning the immigrant to the old country. The fear of trachoma was so great that mothers often blindfolded their children during the long Atlantic Ocean voyage to prevent any eye irritation.

In truth, the numbers denied admissions were small. In 1911, a typical year, 749,642 aliens were examined at Ellis Island; 16,910 (2.3 percent) were turned down for medical reasons, and only 1,167 of these because of trachoma.

Despite all these precautions, trachoma found its way into the elementary schools of Manhattan. By 1912 about 20 percent of children in some classes exhibited the early signs of the disease. In one month, 12,647 children were sent home because of trachoma. (Other reasons included head lice, diphtheria, scabies and ringworm.) Through rigorous hygienic measures the incidence of trachoma rapidly diminished and by 1920 it was no longer a public health threat. The last resident cases of trachoma in this country were found amongst the poorer enclaves of Appalachia and on some Native American reservations.

Blindness was well known to the ancients. Indeed, it was the most obvious and the most troublesome of the many medical afflictions burdening primitive societies. Genesis tells us that when Isaac was old, "his eyes were too dim to see." And it was the blindness of his eyes rather than the blindness of his heart that led him to bestow his patrimony upon Jacob. And when Jacob was old, he too knew the encumbrance of blindness. Yet while the Bible frequently associates loss of vision with aging, it is silent on the subject of blindness in childhood.

An ancient Egyptian parchment, dating back to 1,500 BCE and referred to as the Ebers papyrus, describes a clinically distinct disease of childhood characterized by intense irritation, redness and watering of the eyes; in time, the conjunctival surfaces become painful and visibly rough and granular; eventually the victim's vision fails. Some 16 centuries later, the Greek physician Dioscorides named the disease trachoma from a Greek word meaning rough.

Roman physicians declared that the disease was endemic to the children of the Middle East; and the movement of Roman troops and administrators between Rome and its more southerly colonies brought trachoma to southern Europe. And while trachoma was then equated with poverty, such well-established personages as the great Cicero were victims of trachoma.

There is little mention of trachoma in the ensuing centuries until the 13th century. Trachoma was again evident in the cities of southern Europe, brought back by the Crusaders. Indeed, each time European armies invaded the Middle East, trachoma reappeared in Europe. Napoleon's armies swarmed over Egypt in the early years of the 19th century; and over one-fourth of the French troops contracted trachoma and were made unfit for further military duty. The French called it Egyptian ophthalmia.

Trachoma continued to flourish in the crowded urban centers of Africa and Asia; and while it disappeared in European middle class communities, it lingered in the ghettoes and *shtetls*.

For those American Jews who made the transition from the old country to the *goldeneh medina*, the bitter memory of trachoma will persist.

In the tenements, health was precarious

From the outside, all old tenements look alike: drab, frail and uninviting. And even on the inside their poorly lit corridors seem indistinguishable, differing only in the amount of graffiti, the noise-intensity of the screaming children and the inescapable cooking odors from each apartment. These buildings all share the sour stench of poverty, like escaping sewer gas, which permeated each of their floors.

But a tenement structure is more than a relic of 19th-century architecture designed to teach occupants the extent to which they can survive without fresh air. Each squalid tenement represents an involuntary community of extended, first-generation families crowded together by circumstances beyond their control. With five apartments per floor and a minimum of six residents in each flat, a tenement becomes the enforced residence for about 200 souls varying in age from imperiled infancy to the feeble elderly – a small village with neither mayor nor police force to adjudicate disputes between tenants.

Noise was the constant accompaniment of life in the tenements. Parents did not talk to each other, they yelled; children did not converse, they screamed; and doors were never closed, they were slammed. Even the hours preceding dawn were bereft of silence, for this was the time when workers on the night-shift returned from their labors and others were awakening to drive their wagons or stock their pushcarts unto the busy streets. Other communities had tolling bells to signify terrible or awesome happenings; but the tenements, filled with Jewish families, had only silence to announce such events. Silence, like unbidden telegrams, spoke eloquently of disaster or grief. Thus, the building silenced itself on Yom Kippur or whenever there was serious illness or impending death somewhere in its midst.

Consider now a Brooklyn tenement somewhere on Vermont Avenue and sometime in 1928. On the third floor front there lived a struggling family called the Silversteins, an average household consisting of the parents, a surviving grandmother, one unmarried aunt and four children all below the age of 10. Old man Silverstein – he was hovering at about age 40 – worked as a cutter in a garment factory and looked as though he had modeled for a Dickens novel on sweat shops. Mrs. Silverstein, worn down by life at age 35, cooked, cleaned and seemed in eternal mourning. Her mother, known to the rest of the tenement as *Bubba*, brooded quietly by the front window inspecting the ebb and flow of human traffic below. The maiden aunt, the mother's younger sister, always silent, worked somewhere in town but no one knew the nature of her labors. And the four children, three girls and a boy, were learning the various defenses needed for urban survival.

A Sunday in early spring, a working day in the dense Jewish neighborhood of Brownsville, but not for old man Silverstein, whose given name was known only to his wife and his Creator. He customarily was dressed in drab gray working clothes as he rushed down the stairs to go, each daybreak, to the subway entrance. But not on this Sunday; nor were there the usual household noises that bespoke of activity within. Just silence. Later in the morning an automobile parked in front of the tenement and an unsmiling man wearing a suit, tie and neat overcoat entered the building. Clearly, he was a physician since he carried the identifying black bag and he owned a car. He entered the Silverstein flat while the other third-floor occupants peered anxiously through partially opened doors.

Hours passed and the aura of silence which began in the Silverstein apartment had now spread through the entire tenement. Children who normally spoke only in screams now subdued their yelling; and silence, like contagion, spread from floor to floor. The doctor was still there while the older boys of the neighborhood, more interested in modern conveyances, began to circle his car speculating about the mysteries of internal combustion engines and such strange external items as windshield wipers.

At one point, the doctor left and rushed to the corner drugstore to make a rapid telephone call. And about another hour passed when a black van arrived and two uniformed men ascended to the third floor carrying a portable stretcher. They soon emerged from the Silverstein apartment carrying one of the children on their stretcher; and the fate of this little girl was obvious since the sheet covered her face.

The little Silverstein child had died of a terrible disease called diphtheria, a disease nurtured in places of poverty. Before the preventive immunization programs, diphtheria had been a constant menace to the inner city youngsters, carrying a 25 percent mortality rate. But since the year 2000, this nation has witnessed only three cases of diphtheria, all in immigrant children.

For the Jews of America, the tenement era is now confined to the wondrous recollections of I. B. Singer and to the murmurings of their grandparents; but there is a newer generation of non-Jewish immigrants, now packed in urban slums and who are just as vulnerable to the diseases of poverty as were the Jews, their predecessors.

Photo courtesy Dr. K. Korr

A Jewish immigrant family from Austria-Hungary posed for a departure photograph. Their names were popular in the early 1900s in Jewish families. In front row are Harry and Irving; mother Rachel holds baby David; the two girls are cousins Hannah and Sadie, who stayed behind with their grandparents, seated.

Naming a Jewish child:
A century of Jewish names in R.I.

Conferring a first name on a Jewish child is not to be undertaken carelessly or frivolously. It often involves extended, sometimes divisive, family discussion beginning months before the anticipated birth date. And, before the days of gender-identifying sonography, both a male and a female name needed to be selected.

Since the name chosen represents the first gift that the parents bestow on their newborn, it merits serious study. The ultimate choice will represent a compromise among many discordant and reconciling pressures. On the one hand, there are religious traditions, and, on the other, assimilationist pressures favoring currently fashionable names such as Tiffany or Cody, which would bewilder the most tolerant of rabbis.

During the course of earlier studies attempting to define institutional usage in bygone times, an opportunity arose to compile a substantial list of first names of Jews dying in Rhode Island during the early decades of the 20th century, a population largely born overseas. Through the auspices of the two Rhode Island funeral establishments which had historically fulfilled the mortuary needs of the local Jewish community, 22,646 given names (11,717 females and 10, 929 males) were provided from these certificates. The dates of birth covered about a century of records from 1849 to 1959.

These names were first sorted by gender, date and place of birth. In each category the names were counted and placed in order of frequency. The study then attempted to determine whether this ranking exhibited any trends in relation to the times and places of birth; and, when meaningful shifts were documented, whether there were explanations for such changes. (A more extensive compilation of these retrospective studies may be found in *Rhode Island Jewish Historical Notes: Vol. 12, No. 2, Nov., 1996.*)

The most frequently chosen names for girls were: Sarah, Ann, Rose, Ida, Bessie, Fannie and Rebecca (for those born in Russia-Poland); Ann, Rose, Rebecca, Sarah, Esther and Fannie (Austria-Hungary); Sarah,

Ann, Rose, Bertha, Hannah and Fannie (Western Europe), and Rose, Ann, Lillian, Jennie, Sarah and Ida (U.S.).

For boys: Samuel, Abraham, Jacob, Morris, Louis and Joseph (Russia-Poland); Samuel, Morris, Jacob, Abraham, Louis and Max (Austria-Hungary); Jacob, Isaac, Louis, Samuel, Joseph and Max (Western Europe) and Samuel, Harry, Louis, Joseph, Abraham and David (U.S.).

As American Jews have become increasingly assimilated, name preferences for their offspring have broadened and now incorporate names that had previously been shunned by Jewish families. Among male Jews born in Russia-Poland, particularly before 1900, there had been few with the names of the tsars, (Peter, Paul, Ivan, Nicholas). The major apostolic names (Matthew, Mark, Luke, John, Peter, Paul) were similarly avoided.

Jews, in general, did not name their children after historical tyrants. There were not many Jewish Alexanders or Napoleons.

Some names, such as Max, Irving, Hyman, Bernard, Louis and Morris were commonly chosen in the late 19th and early 20th centuries (up to 24.4 percent, depending on place of birth). Indeed, they were selected so often that they have now assumed a distinctly Semitic aura. Yet not one of these names is of Hebraic or Yiddish origin; most of them are derived from Latin, Old High German or Anglo-Saxon. The name Morris, or its variants Moritz or Maurice, appeared 615 times amongst the 11,717 male Jewish names. Morris was the dominant choice of those born in Russia-Poland, Moritz was confined almost exclusively to Jews born in Austria-Hungary, while Maurice was more common among those born in Western Europe or the United States.

When the names in this cohort of 22,646 are examined against the decade and place of birth, three realities emerge. Firstly, there is a progressive widening of choices from the mid-19th to the mid-20th century, and moving west from the Pale of Russia to the Western nations. Secondly, the use of distinctly Yiddish names, such as *Menachim, Simcha, Motke, Feivel, Peshe, Rivka*, or *Basha* have virtually disappeared; along with the Hebrew names of animals, *Hersh, Lieb, Leo, Dov, Barnet*, or adjectival names such as *Fruma, Shayna*, and *Blima*. Thirdly, the use of non-Jewish names has greatly expanded.

Given the immense societal pressures to conform, it seemed unlikely that an analysis of the relatively large collection of Jewish first names would yield much beyond the relative frequencies of the various scriptural names: patriarchs, judges, prophets, kings, or archangels.

Surprisingly, some modest trends do emerge which reflect the unique experiences and involuntary migrations of the Diaspora communities. There is an increasingly diversified and imaginative choice of first names by Jewish parents in the current era. American Jews are now using many names of Celtic and Gaelic origin (Kevin, Scott, Sean (or Shawn), Kelly, Megan, Erin.) Nonetheless — no matter what compelling choices are derived from the secular *zeitgeist* — never has the frequency of time-honored Jewish names, e.g., Sarah, Abraham, David, in any of the analyzed Jewish groups diminished below 25 percent.

A good name, says Proverbs, is rather to be chosen than great riches.

Let only the elderly judge the elderly

Rhode Island is becoming progressively older as more of its citizens have long since seen their 65th birthdays. How do society, and perhaps some of its younger physicians, view the lingering elderly? With ambivalence, certainly: Sometimes they are viewed as honored, wise and deserving of respect and help; at other times as useless burdens on the greater community.

Society employs many names in portraying its elderly, many of them abusive and demeaning. The backgrounds of the more degrading terms are worth exploring.

Hag: Probably derived from the Greek word *hagia* meaning holy or saintly (as in the word *hagiography*), but by the 16th century, (and then spelled *hegge*) it signified an elderly, ugly female. A 1552 text declares: "Hegges or night furys, or wytches like unto olde women which do suck the bloude of children in the nyght." And in Macbeth we encounter "secret, black and midnight hags." Somehow over the centuries, the hag has been transformed from a wise elder to a dreaded servant of Satan.

Coot: Colloquially, the word depicts a querulous, crotchety old male. Technically, however, the word describes a web-footed, aquatic diving bird (*Fulica Americana*) with a bill extending upwards between its eyes to cover its anterior skull. Thus, from a distance, the bird appears bald. So the coot became symbolic of baldness, gracelessness and, finally, foolishness. These attributes were then transferred to the elderly male. In truth, quite a number of birds have become metaphors for the elderly male, for example, "old buzzard," "old crow," and "old coot."

Crone: The term describes an elderly, withered woman which may have descended from an Anglo-Saxon word, *croonie,* meaning an old, toothless ewe. The crone, in some earlier cultures, has been described as both giver and taker of life, the guardian of medicinal secrets and midwifery, but also the embodiment of decay and witchcraft.

Crock: A common word for a senile patient with multiple medical problems, few of them amenable to effective treatment. The symbol of a fragile piece of crockery is emblematic of the frail elderly in many cultures.

Father Time: This is a confusing pastiche of many intertwining myths incorporating such symbols of impending death as the hourglass and the scythe. In medieval art the cloaked male figure was frequently associated with *ourobos* (a winged snake devouring its tail), which is a wheel-like symbol representing the cycle of birth and death. The grim reaper image is traced to Chronos (or Saturn), oldest of the Greco-Roman gods and the father of Zeus. Saturn, the most distant planet visible to the eye, is depicted astrologically as remote, sluggish, baleful, gloomy and elderly.

There are many inanimate objects that symbolize the finiteness of life. In Ecclesiastes the metaphors for death include the snapped silver cord, the broken golden bowl, the shattered pitcher and the wheel broken at the well. In societies that perceive life and death as recurrent elements in a dynamic cycle, the wheel is a frequent symbol.

Yet other common emblems of the terminal years of life include hour-glasses and candles. Somehow, though, these metaphors do not convey the same sense of the malevolent, shriveled soul who exercises a distinct threat to the young and vigorous, as do such terms as hag. Nor do they evoke a sense of uselessness as do terms such as crock or coot.

Gomer: Biblical scholars will remember that Gomer was a grandson of Noah. Many semanticists may recall the Teutonic word *gome,* meaning old man, possibly cognate with the Latin word *homo,* meaning man. But, in truth, "GOMER" is an acronym representing the first letters of the pejorative phrase, "Get Out of My Emergency Room." It was probably coined by some hassled emergency room officer (or TV script writer) who desperately needed a euphemism to hide his frustration when confronted with yet another irresolvable medical admission at 3 a.m.

Words such as crone and hag, when viewed in isolation, are insensitive and degrading. Hostile expressions such as these are more commonly voiced by overburdened health care personnel who feel helpless when confronting human decay that they can neither slow nor reverse.

Old people, said the poet Goethe, should be judged solely by old people. This necessary instruction might also be augmented by the immortal poetry of Ogden Nash:

> *Senescence begins*
> *And middle age ends*
> *The day your descendants*
> *Outnumber your friends.*

Dr. Stanley Aronson's portrait of his immigrant grandmother, Ethel Hassner (1885-1935).

We're a people in perpetual transition

Commentaries on transnational Jewish migrations

I t can be a luxury cruise, perhaps to the West Indies; a prison ship carrying England's excess prison population to the Australian penal colony; even a trip in a hell called steerage, bearing desperate European refugees westward across the Atlantic. The tourists, the prisoners and the refugees were all marine travelers, but only one sailed voluntarily.

The Jews have never been a maritime nation. Yet the magnitude of their global dissemination in the 19th and 20th centuries remains unique

> *And, can you imagine an American Jew, derived from some godforsaken, pogrom-ridden village, talking nostalgically of the Motherland while praising the cultural authenticity and tolerance of Tsarist Russia?*

amongst the many identified ethnic groups constituting the immigrant American population. No definable population has undergone such extensive migration while still preserving its cultural integrity.

In recent centuries, every European nation had sent its excess population elsewhere, principally to the Western Hemisphere. And thus, while Ireland, for example, sent many to the West, largely impelled by over-population and the potato famine of the mid-19th century; and Italy, undergoing civil unrest, dispatched its young people to North and South America, Ireland and Italy nonetheless remained steadfastly the cultural and political locus of things called Italian or Irish.

And both nations persisted as motherlands for their overseas descendants. Generations later, many an American of Irish or Italian descent makes nostalgic pilgrimages to the motherland; and, between 1908 and 1925, 1.16 million Italians living in the United States emigrated permanently back to Italy, representing 55.8 percent of all who had originally come to this nation.

Jewish migration to other lands, principally the United States, was prompted by different forces, and was more numeric in terms of the migrating percent of the resident population. It resulted ultimately in irreversible changes in the cultural and demographic profile of global Jewry.

Furthermore, the number of migrating Jews who ever returned to their European countries of origin remains extremely small.

And, can you imagine an American Jew, derived from some godforsaken, pogrom-ridden village, talking nostalgically of the Motherland while praising the cultural authenticity and tolerance of Tsarist Russia?

Further, can you picture this assimilated Jew saying to himself: "Yes, I am an American, but part of my heritage belongs forever to Minsk."

Migration of Jews to overseas continents began in earnest in the middle of the 19th century. Which is not to say that some Jews did not undertake hazardous ocean voyages to the Americas as early as the 18th century. This migratory process by 1940 culminated in the collective transfer of some 4 million European Jews to the United States. Newport, R.I., by 1750, had the largest Jewish community in North America numbering almost 1,000 members of what was then called the Mosaic Faith.

Most of those Jews were of Sephardic origin and represented groups grown robust in overcoming the travails of migration. They had been expelled from Spain and Portugal, had migrated to Holland or Morocco or even Tunisia; and because of inhospitable circumstances, were then forced to voyage to Dutch West Indian colonies such as Curacao, where the long arm of the Iberian Inquisition finally caught up with them, forcing yet another migration, this time to a Rhode Island refuge.

Jews had dreamed of a major migration to the Americas as early as 1783. In June of that year, the Jews of Frankfort and Leipzig sent a prayerful letter to the president of the Continental Congress: "*Schreiben eines deutschen Juden an den Amerikanischen Presidenten.*"

Part of the letter declared: "We ask no more than to be permitted to become subjects of these 13 provinces, and would gladly contribute twofold taxes for their benefit, if we can only obtain permission to establish colonies at our own cost and to engage in agriculture, commerce, arts and sciences." The proposal was not answered.

To an 18th-century Jewish family sequestered in some small Russian village surrounded by seamless poverty, America was at best a delusory dream.

These Jews, to a substantial degree illiterate in the dominant languages of the continent, had no way of undertaking passage to the west. The living conditions of the Eastern European Jews were indeed so perilous that President Grant, commenting specifically on the Rumanian enclaves of Jewry, declared: "The reports concerning the sufferings of the Rumanian Jews deeply stir our humane sentiments. That which reaches us from Rumania is a chain of malice and barbarity without measure."

Within a century, however, a new diaspora transformed Judaism. And, in this demographic transformation Europe was no longer the center of global Jewry and the United States, and to a lesser degree, Israel, became the new nucleus of Judaism.

The reasons for this massive Jewish migration can be readily summarized in four principal themes: First, and foremost, were the egregious living conditions, and lack of meaningful medical resources, in Eastern Europe.

Second was the lack of commercial opportunity or educational advancement in Eastern Europe, particularly with established quotas for all secondary and tertiary forms of education in the Pale of Settlement.

Third was the unrestricted immigration policy and the expansion of industrial opportunities in the United States eagerly seeking workers.

And fourth were the many letters from immigrants, already established in the United States, extolling life in the land of golden opportunity and expressing a desire to subsidize the transatlantic passage for those still festering in the old country.

My next two columns will address the specific demographic numbers underlying this massive migration and touch upon some of the medical problems that the Jewish immigrants had encountered in passage.

The nature of migration

A people in perpetual transition

The first hasty emigration, I suppose, was the expulsion of Adam and Eve from the Garden of Eden. They, and their progeny, were then banished to lead lives of struggle and travail in hard-scrabble territories east of Eden.

It is claimed, though, that when they departed, Adam had whispered to Eve: "We live in an age of transition, my dear."

However, the first truly transcontinental Judaic Diaspora, the Roman expulsion of the Jews to Europe, dispersed the human remnants of a small, cohesive Middle Eastern nation, already educated in the rigors of displacement by the Babylonian exile.

The enforced transplantation of many Jews to pagan Europe – to southern Gaul and the Rhine valley – changed forever the character of Judaism, altering it from a regional sect to a globally distributed religion. Change – sometimes painful, sometimes beneficial – has since been its lingering inheritance.

Emigration – abandoning one's home, one's village, one's motherland – is a wrenching experience; a venture not to be initiated lightly. Emigration to a strange and forbidding land may sound adventuresome but for a frightened family with no tangible resources, no reliable knowledge about America except for fanciful myths, and no guarantee of future livelihood, emigration to the unknown requires a steely resolve and consummate courage.

It is true that most Jews leaving Eastern Europe during the last decades of the 19th century departed involuntarily to escape the burden of relentless pogroms.

Still, it was a fateful choice between staying behind and surviving under further brutality and poverty, on the one hand, or encountering an alien climate and the unknown on the other.

In the five fateful decades between 1870 and 1920, 4.3 million Jews left their ancestral homes in Eastern Europe to venture to new lands, largely in the Western Hemisphere and specifically to the United States.

An old platitude declares, that for every door that closes, another swings open. Perhaps, but not necessarily in the same place nor at the same time.

And, many a family that had their village door slammed shut found no congenial door to welcome them. It must be emphasized that this great Jewish scattering was but a small part of the movement of some 65 million Europeans migrating to the Western Hemisphere during the interval between 1810 and 1940, the Era of Great Dispersion.

There were, however, notable demographic differences. Only a splinter of the resident Irish, Italians, Scottish or English (the dominant emigrant groups) traveled west; and for the most part these nations sent only their youngest, most creative and healthiest children to the Americas. The Jews of Europe, on the other hand, sent their families – young, old and infirm – leaving only a dispirited remnant behind. And when the Great Dispersion was ended by World War II, the demographic center of Judaism was no longer Eastern Europe but was now the United States.

In the words of the historian Jacob Lestschinsky: "The United States is an English country in language only; it does not belong to the English people. Nationhood is a much broader concept than language."

By the numbers

Consider the following numbers: In 1840 there were an estimated 3.9 million Jews living in Europe constituting 87.8 percent of world Jewry.

In the same year there were about 50,000 Jews in the United States, about 1.1 percent of world Jewry. By 1945 there were three million Jews still in Europe (down from about 9.9 million in 1932). In the United States there now were six million Jews constituting 54.6 percent of world Jewry. The center of Judaic life was now west of the Atlantic.

Where else had the Eastern European Jews migrated in the century between 1840 and 1940? Canada absorbed 153,000; Argentina, about 224,000; Brazil, about 71,000 and other Latin American countries (including Cuba) about 59,000. South Africa took in some 76,000 Jews (largely from the Baltic countries and particularly Lithuania).

And, the British Mandate in Palestine absorbed 379,000 European Jews in the century preceding World War II. The greatest number migrating to Palestine, according to British records, was 147,502 between the years 1931 and 1935.

Prior to 1914, Jewish emigration from Tsarist Russia sometimes required the help of smugglers to get beyond the border guards, but the gates to the United States were open wide except for those with certain specified diseases such as tuberculosis or trachoma, those exhibiting mental deficiency, and those alleged to hold anarchistic or communist beliefs.

Following World War I (1914-1918), entrance to the United States became increasingly restricted as exemplified by the Immigration Act of 1924, which favored migration from northwestern Europe (Britain and Scandanavia) while curtailing migration from southeastern (Mediterranean and Slavic nations) Europe.

As for the health and well-being of those Jews transplanted to the New World? *See next chapter.*

Beyond the airbrushed history of immigration

Failure was as common as success in the new country

The customary story, appealing in its nostalgic embellishments, runs something like this: There once was a Polish-Jewish family composed of a Talmud-reading father who had longed to be a philosopher but was required by circumstance to eke out a meager living as a tailor; a mother with the strength of a prophetess, the vision of an eagle and the tenacity of a tiger; two pre-adolescent sons and a 14-year-old daughter, selfless and a part-time surrogate mother to her brothers, all living congenially in a modest *shtetl*.

Circumstances deteriorated in 1893 and the family abandoned their simple home to venture west to the land of milk and honey beyond the Atlantic Ocean. After much travail the family reached the port city of Hamburg and embarked upon a steamer headed for the port of New York.

After a turbulent voyage of 29 days, confined for the most part to steerage, they arrived in New York, passed through a forbidding place called Ellis Island, were met by the mother's brother (who had emigrated to America the previous year) and were then settled in a dreary tenement apartment on Eldridge Street in the Lower East Side of Manhattan.

The father found employment in a sweatshop making aprons, but after five years he had saved sufficient funds to open a small store of his own making and selling women's apparel.

He and his wife strove to enlarge the business; and within 10 years they managed three profitable stores selling women's clothing and accessories. When they finally retired (to live in Boca Raton, Fla.) they were the proud owners of a chain of stores in New York and its suburbs.

And the children? Both boys attended City College; and one became a prominent lawyer living in a Westchester suburb and the other an acclaimed surgeon practicing in New York's Mt. Sinai Hospital.

The daughter, an alumna of Barnard College, was a widely acclaimed author of sociology texts and a professor at Radcliffe College in

Massachusetts. And, to this day, the family foundation still underwrites community-based self-help programs.

Sounds familiar; and indeed the scenario faithfully abides by life's realities – in many instances, but not always. It neglects to mention – or document for those who insist upon the balanced truth – the many times where America's open door did not lead to wealth, social status and success but rather to disillusionment, betrayal, abandonment, sickness and despair.

Without lessening the indomitable courage and the creative opportunism of the emigrant Jews, one cannot ignore the large number of mental breakdowns – even suicides - amongst early immigrants before the availability of such support resources as the Visiting Nurse Service and the educational alliances had been established to give advice and practical training to those in need of both.

Desperate lives

The lives of the Jewish immigrants seeking a new way of living in the Lower East Side were littered with instances of serious emotional disorders, of desperate fathers abandoning their families, of adolescents – persuaded by the life style of their non-Jewish classmates – showing embarrassment by the "old ways" of their parents and enmity to all things Jewish.

And, if one doubts these verities, a review of the inner pages of the Jewish daily newspaper, The Forward, during the early decades of the 20th century, will become an illuminating exercise.

A column, called *"Bintel Briefs"* – a bundle of letters – published the anguished outcries of mothers, with infant children and no source of income, abandoned by their husbands. And fathers in utter despair for want of a job; unmarried women crying out for the privilege of a college education, but required to work in some sweat-shop in order to allow their brothers to attend a university; domestic violence, both verbal and physical; and mothers appealing to the unknown or the unknowable for a miracle to stave off the mortal diseases afflicting their infants or the inner city depravities threatening their adolescents.

For every success story proclaimed loudly in the marketplaces of Hester Street or Delancey Street there were a dozen failures whispered furtively in the tenement hallways, with fathers sometimes muttering in Yiddish, "Why did we ever leave Poland?"

And, for every successful venture into the capricious world of capitalism, there were a handful of earnest Jewish workers who allied themselves with one form of socialism or another because of the inherent injustices in the marketplace economic system conjoined with their personal failure to rise above the menial nature of their jobs.

Airbrushed history teaches us that the critical years following immigration were times when iconic Jewish mothers compiled ranked occupations for their infant sons (first a physician, second a lawyer, third a high-school teacher) while whispering prayers that their infant daughters would marry well.

More likely, the immigrant mother's prayers were oriented toward more meaningful issues such as her husband's job security, her sister's failing health (is it, God forbid, consumption?), the curtains for the front window or whether she will be able to pay this month's rent on time.

Chapter 5

There were giants in those days

G iants, in most cultures, have been beheld with justifiable hostility and understandable fear. Typically, they were portrayed as lawless, amoral and destructive creatures. But, according to ancient legends, the race of giants, with the help of the gods, was finally exiled, restrained beneath mountains or vanquished in combat. A few escaped, however, to roam the earth wreaking vengeance and mayhem.

On rare occasions a valiant human, with virtuous spirit, confronted one of these ogres and slew him in mortal battle. (In the many folktales of marauding giants, there is little mention of any female giants, which may account in part for the paucity of their numbers.)

The Hebrews, too, acknowledged that in antediluvian days there were giants, the Nephilim, populating the earth (Gen. 6:4).

During the years following the Exodus, Moses sent scouts to survey Canaan and its neighboring lands. After 40 days the scouts returned and reported that much of the territory was occupied by the race of Nephilim and the Anakites, terrifying warriors of gigantic proportions (Numb.13: 25-33). Joshua overcame the apprehensions of the Israelites and led them to victory over the Anakites. There is later mention that the lands of the Anakites were then assigned to the descendants of Lot (Deut. 2:10-19).

The first explicit Scriptural description of an encounter with a giant appears in the first book of Samuel. The Philistines had assembled their forces for battle against the men of Israel led by Saul. The two armies opposed each other from two hilltops overlooking the intervening valley of Elah. Each morning for 40 days, a champion of the Philistines, Goliath of Gath, stepped forward to challenge in mortal combat any representative of Israel (I Samuel 17: 1-50). Goliath, a Semitic name meaning splendor, was said to be six cubits and a hand span, over 10 feet tall. Tradition declares that a remnant of the giants had taken refuge with the Philistines after their bloody encounter with the Ammonites.

No soldier of Saul's army volunteered to face Goliath in single battle. But then the youngest son of Jesse the Ephrathite, a lad named David, who tended the family's sheep, stepped forward and said to Saul: "Let no man's courage fail him. Your servant will go and fight this Philistine." And so the youthful David confronted the giant Goliath in the valley of Elah. David then removed a stone from his pouch and, propelling it with his sling, struck the giant's forehead and thus killed him. The Philistines, seeing their champion dead, fled in disarray.

The encounter between David and Goliath has been preserved as a metaphor of the eternal contest between righteousness and evil, the battle between a lightly armed but resolute youth, pure of heart, vanquishing a giant who is impelled solely by murderous intent. It is a legend which resonates in all cultures whenever a brave young soul confronts the neighborhood bully. It is a legend, too, which moved David from the anonymous ranks of shepherds to the throne of Israel and to his ultimate role in history as the progenitor of kings.

But might there be an alternate explanation for David's miraculous victory over an armored giant? And how could a veteran warrior such as Goliath have allowed himself to be exposed to a youth bearing a slingshot? Is it possible, then, that Goliath's vision was defective?

The need to question arises in all ethnic groups and cultures, but amongst Jews it becomes an obsession. And so, inevitably, skepticism has arisen concerning the underlying details of this ostensibly one-sided encounter.

Nordic and Hellenic mythology claim that giants were derived from a race clearly distinguishable from humans. Hebrew *midrash*, however, declares that Goliath's mother was Oprah, a Moabite woman related to Ruth. And thus if Goliath's lineage was at least partly human, might he not then be vulnerable to human diseases? More specifically, might there be a disease that can convert a human into an intimidating giant with a thunderous voice while simultaneously burdening him with an increasingly defective vision?

Humans, on rare occasions, have been known to exceed eight feet in height. Most of these giants, however, have been victims of a pituitary gland disease characterized by an overproduction of growth hormone. And if this pathological process begins beyond puberty the disease is called acromegaly.

Acromegalics are rare, with an estimated 300 new cases per year in the United States. The typical acromegalic is a hulking giant of simian proportions with overgrown hands and feet; his voice is booming and resonant; his face is coarsely grained; his barrel-shaped chest is excessively hairy; his forehead is unusually prominent and his jaws are abnormally protuberant giving him the appearance of belligerent ferocity. But the underlying glandular disease makes this giant excessively weak, his bones much more fragile than normal (and hence, more susceptible to projectiles such as sling shots), and his vision often defective, as the pituitary gland overgrowth impinges upon the optic nerves.

In ancient days there may have been a race of giants terrorizing mankind. Scientists, however, declare that there is no archeological evidence, no recovered bones, to support the contention that giants had once roamed the earth before the great flood. The race of giants has therefore been reduced to fanciful legend. But it is still possible that a rare individual, made huge because of a growth-promoting glandular abnormality, may have been recruited as the warrior-champion of some army. And if Goliath did indeed have an endocrinological disease such as acromegaly he would have been chosen more for his forbidding appearance than his battle-proven prowess.

Goliath's hypothesized vulnerability, however, was unknown to David, and this youth's act of bravery, therefore, stands undiminished.

A time of testing, a time of punishment

Preponderance of the number 40

During the turbulent 14th century, the Italian peninsula was witness to intermittent warfare, a succession of pestilences and periodic crop failures; but none of these tragedies compared with the devastation wrought by the arrival of the bubonic plague, the Black Death, in the year, 1347.

Italian authorities understood that certain infectious diseases were communicable. They also appreciated the value of isolating the newly infected patient so as to protect the remaining population. But for how many days should this interval of isolation last?

Since physicians knew nothing then of the germ theory of disease nor the mechanisms by which infectious pathogens were spread, they turned necessarily to the Scriptures for counsel. The Book of Leviticus prescribed certain intervals of isolation for those afflicted with skin diseases said to be "unclean," usually specifying the time in multiples of seven days. Seven or 14 days, however, seemed an inadequate time. But a further review of the Scriptures, both Hebrew and Christian, brought to light a particular number appearing many times, and with each mention it defined an interval of profound significance. The number was 40.

Accordingly, the Italian public health officials assigned the number 40 to the days that any plague victim was to be physically separated from the others (*una quarantina di giorni*, 40 days). and thus was born the English word, quarantine.

The first Scriptural mention of 40 occurs when the Lord declares to Noah, "I will make it rain upon the earth for 40 days and 40 nights, and I will blot out from the earth all existence that I created." (Genesis 7:4). The number 40 is mentioned twice more in Genesis first when Abraham pleads with the Lord not to destroy the occupants of Sodom; and again when Joseph orders his physicians to embalm the body of his father, Israel. "It required 40 days which is the full period for embalming." (Genesis 50:3).

The duration of the long trek from the Sea of Reeds through the wilderness of Sinai is described as 40 years. "I brought you up from the land of Egypt and led you through the wilderness for 40 years." (Amos 2:10). Berating the house of Israel, the Lord said, "Did you offer sacrifice and oblation to Me, those 40 years in the wilderness?" (Amos 5: 25). Until they came to the borders of Canaan "...the Israelites ate manna for 40 years." (Exodus 16:35). When Moses was bidden to approach the Lord to receive the stone tablets on Mount Sinai, the Scriptures relate "...and Moses remained on the mountain 40 days and 40 nights." (Exodus 24:18). In yet another passage, Moses is described as eating no bread and drinking no water for 40 days and 40 nights while writing the terms of the covenant upon the tablets (Exodus 34: 28.1). As Canaan was approached, Moses sent forth scouts to survey the land. "At the end of 40 days they returned." (Numbers 14: 33-35).

Even the plans to construct the tabernacle define the number of silver sockets to be 40 (Exodus 26: 19-25).

The tenure in office seems to have been, almost uniformly, 40 years. Eli had been chieftain of Israel for 40 years (I Samuel 4: 18). When the prophetess, Deborah, led Israel, "the land was tranquil for 40 years." (Judges 5: 3 1). And in the days before the kings, Othriel the Kennizite, ruled in peace for 40 years (Judges 3: 11). "Saul, the son of Kish, a man of the tribe of Benjamin, who reigned for 40 years." (Acts 13: 21). David reigned as king for 40 years (II Samuel 5: 4). "The length of Solomon's reign was 40 years." (I Kings 11: 42).

And on other occasions when a time interval needed to be specified, 40 was frequently chosen. It was "after 40 years had passed" when Moses was confronted with the burning bush in the desert before Mount Sinai and thus the onset of his prophetic role. Jonah proclaimed the word of the Lord: "Forty days more and Nineveh shall be overcome." (Jonah 3: 4). The Lord said: "For 40 years I will make the land of Egypt the most desolate of desolate lands." (Ezekiel 29:11-13). Caleb, when speaking to Joshua, says, "I was 40 years old when Moses the servant of the Lord sent me from Kadesh-barnea to spy out the land." Even the length of the great hall of the Temple was 40 cubits (Ezekiel 41: 2.1).

Was 40 a number meaningful solely to the Hebrews? The New Testament declares that Jesus was led away by the Spirit into the wilderness, to be tempted by the devil. "For 40 days and nights he fasted." (Matthew 4: 2). And after the risen Jesus had returned from his tomb, "...over a period of 40 days he appeared" before the time of

Ascension (Acts 1: 3). Both Buddha and Mohammed began their sacred missions at age 40.

The Athenian corps of judges numbered 40 as did the illustrious membership of the French Academy, "the immortal forty."

The biblical 40 appears to define critical intervals of expectation, of punishment and contrition, and of maturation; but also intervals of intense travail, introspection and renewal, and even the length of service in office.

But still, why 40? Why not 39 or 50? Is 40 intrinsically more holy than other numerals? Is there any tangible thing in the natural world, in the skies above, or even within the human body which consistently numbers 40? Man has been endowed with 10 fingers and 10 toes which add up only to 20 digits. But, the Hebrews remembered, they had been created in God's image, and hence it must be presumed that God, too, has 20 digits. Therefore, what better way of proclaiming the devotional union between man and his God, than by exalting and perpetuating the number 40?

Even those unfamiliar with the Bible confer special attributes upon the numeral 40. "Life begins at 40," some say; others, concerned about diet, might fear being "fair, fat and 40." And to Shakespeare, 40 years of age was a cold and distant shore when senility began: "When 40 winters shall besiege thy brow, And dig deep trenches in thy beauty's field."

Whether it defines the interval of quarantine, the years of servitude in the deserts of Sinai, the reigning duration over a fractious people, a prophetic cipher, or even when gall bladder problems often begin, 40 remains a wondrous number, filled with majesty and mystery.

The story of Drs. Tay and Sachs

B efore a laboratory test to identify parent-carriers of Tay-Sachs
Disease (TSD) had been devised, the disease had arisen about
once in every 4,000 Ashkenazic Jewish live births. Certainly there were
more commonly encountered causes of infant mortality among Jewish
families, but TSD loomed, historically, as a particularly dreaded ethnic
burden.

The birth and early growth of infants destined to develop TSD was
generally normal. But about the seventh month of life these infants
began to show arrested cerebral development, signs of blindness and
periodic seizures. Death usually came before the end of the second year
of life.

The disease was not described until the 1880s. Undoubtedly it
had existed before, but its clinical singularity went undetected in the
crowded Jewish communities of the East European tsarist pale. Only
when large numbers of Jewish families migrated to the West was TSD
finally recognized as a uniquely hereditary disease of their newborns.

A Scottish physician, Warren Tay, a specialist in diseases of the
eye, practiced medicine in East London. Among the many infants and
children observed by him in his clinic were two infants of "Hebrew
extraction" said to be blind. Tay noted some distinctive changes in the
retinas of these infants and published his ophthalmological findings in
1881.

Across the Atlantic, in 1887, a New York neurologist, Bernard Sachs,
published a more comprehensive paper on the clinical evolution and
underlying pathology of the disease. Eventually he called it amaurotic
family idiocy.

By 1896, Sachs had observed an additional 19 cases, which allowed
him to define the hallmarks of this disorder: It was clearly hereditary,
often afflicting two or more children in the same family. It was invariably
fatal, and all of his patients had been Jewish. (In subsequent years, cases
of TSD were identified in virtually all ethnic populations.)

Bernard Sachs, known to his family and colleagues as Barney,
would have achieved lasting prominence as an outstanding physician

even without his precise portrayal of the terrible hereditary disease that now bears his name.

Sachs's father, Joseph Sachs, was born in a small Bavarian village in 1817. He trained as a schoolteacher in the larger city of Wurzburg; and, in keeping with the established custom within the German-Jewish community, he boarded with one of the local Jewish families. In time, he was attracted to the daughter of this family and they eloped to Hamburg. In 1847, motivated in part to escape the revolutionary turmoil in Western Europe, they sailed for the United States, where Joseph eventually founded a school for boys in Baltimore.

Bernard, one of two male twins, was born Jan. 2, 1858. His twin brother died of scarlet fever close to their fifth birthday. As the Civil War loomed, Joseph Sachs moved his close-knit family to New York, where he established a boarding school that quickly achieved prominence. Barney began his collegiate education at City College of New York, transferring eventually to Harvard, where he received his baccalaureate degree, at the top of his class, in 1878. He was deeply influenced by the newly elaborated theories of evolution advocated in 1859 by Darwin. At age 20, Sachs debated between a career in the biological sciences or one in medicine. And if medicine, which medical school? The Alsatian city of Strasbourg, in 1878, was one of Europe's great centers for the study of medicine. And so Barney sailed for Europe, embarking on an overseas educational interval lasting some six years.

These were intense years for Sachs. He learned medicine from the finest clinicians of Western Europe, but also played his violin, took walking trips through Switzerland and Italy (some in the company of the English poet, Robert Browning) and learned the literary treasures of Europe in their original tongue.

On June 6, 1882, Sachs was awarded his M.D. degree. For two additional years he walked the hospital wards of such hallowed European medical institutions as Vienna's *Algemeine Krankenhaus* (studying with a young Viennese neurologist named Freud), *La Salpetriere* and *Hotel Dieu* in Paris, Charite Hospital in Berlin and the London Hospital.

In May of 1884, young Sachs returned to New York to establish a medical practice eventually confined to diseases of the nervous system. He was appointed to the medical staffs of the Montefiore Home in 1888 and in 1890 became consultant neurologist to Mt. Sinai Hospital.

116

Neurology, at this time, had not yet become an independent medical discipline and Sachs played a prominent role in the professional maturation of this new specialty.

In 1887 Sachs assembled his personal observations on the disease that would eventually bear his name. His inaugural publication on this subject appeared in the September, 1887, issue of the *Journal of Nervous and Mental Disease* with the forbidding title, "On arrested cerebral development with special reference to its cortical pathology."

The paper was a masterpiece of clinical description enriched by the first neuropathological analysis of the disease. This inaugural paper, and a number of succeeding treatises by Sachs, firmly established the disorder as hereditary, distinguishable from others, selectively involving the ganglion cells of the nervous system and found predominantly in Jewish infants of Eastern European extraction.

Sachs also wrote extensively on brain diseases of childhood, particularly such disorders as cerebral palsy, muscular dystrophy and head injuries. In 1895, his great textbook on nervous diseases of childhood appeared, rapidly becoming the standard textbook in the emerging field of pediatric neurology.

In later years, Sachs assumed the editorship of the *Journal of Nervous and Mental Disease*, the presidency of the New York Neurological Society, the presidency of the American Neurological Association and presidency of the first International Congress of Neurology. In the early decades of the 20th century, Sachs worked incessantly as a consultant to various New York hospitals, as professor of neurology at Columbia University's medical school, as a fierce advocate on behalf of infant and child health, and as a philanthropist.

He lived a lengthy and productive life, dying in New York at the age of 82. His terminal years, though, were filled with dread and anxiety as he witnessed the specter of fascism overtaking the many nations of Europe.

In the year of his death, 1940, virtually all of Europe had come under Nazi domination, an isolated England was besieged, the fate of the European Jews was unknown and there was little assurance that this enveloping calamity would be reversed.

What makes a disease Jewish?

In a synagogue class on genealogy some weeks back, a student asked the following question, "Are there Jewish diseases?" A good question, but one which cannot be readily answered. It is a question which gives rise to still further questions. For example, what quality must a disease possess before it can be called Jewish? Certainly if a thousand Jewish youngsters contract measles, that doesn't transform measles into a Jewish disease.

In the broadest sense, diseases may be classified as those which are strictly inherited: the so-called genetic diseases, and those which arise because of some ecological factor, perhaps an infectious agent, an environmental pollutant or even the lack or excess of some dietary component. Of course, these two categories of organic disease - hereditary and environmental - are not mutually exclusive. Certain combinations of genes, not by themselves causative of disease, will nevertheless render their carriers more or less vulnerable to particular extrinsic agents such as viruses.

Let us first consider environmental disease. Prior to 1860, the great majority of Jews survived under primitive circumstances in the Pale of Eastern Europe. Asked then what the "Jewish diseases" were they would have responded, "tuberculosis, typhus, ringworm, trachoma and rickets." Ask the same question of the Jews living on the Lower East Side of Manhattan in the 1930s and their answer would probably have been kidney failure, Buerger's disease, obesity and diabetes. A survey of critical diseases in the Jews of New York and New England today would likely identify cardiovascular disease, Alzheimer's disease and certain forms of cancer as the leading threats to their lives.

Living conditions have drastically altered for American Jews in the past 150 years. The skills of medicine have advanced, the standards of living for American Jews (and their levels of education) have risen dramatically, and accordingly their profiles of illness, as well as their life expectancy have been profoundly altered.

The Jewish population of New York City in the 1920s and '30s was largely working class, living, for the most part, in tenement houses. There certainly was talk then of "Jewish diseases" but there was also a pervasive feeling that denied their existence. The German propaganda apparatus in those days proclaimed the degeneracy of the Jew in appearance, morality, miscegenation and spectrum of illnesses. The American Jews, on the other hand, sought assimilation and the defensive belief that they were indistinguishable from their non-Jewish neighbors. Acknowledging the existence of "Jewish disease" meant a tacit acceptance of the biologic separateness of Jews and perhaps their genetic inferiority.

We now come to the hereditary diseases. After the many diasporas, the forced migrations, the involuntary conversions, the premature loss of lives during the past three millennia and the generations of intermarriage, can there still be some genetic continuity in those who call themselves Jews? There is ample genetic evidence that the current population of Jews shares certain constellations of genes and, as an identifiable ethnic group, is therefore prone to certain illnesses; and some of these genetic clusterings may then lead to lethal diseases.

Consider, as an example, Tay-Sachs Disease (TSD), which is, in the minds of many, the pre-eminent Jewish disease. TSD is what geneticists call a recessive, autosomal disorder. This means it requires both parents to be carriers of the uniquely abnormal gene and that the resultant disease may arise in either male or female offspring of the marital union. A TSD carrier, however, is clinically indistinguishable from a non-carrier. TSD is uniformly fatal, with death occurring well before the fourth birthday.

Is TSD a Jewish disease? It was first described in 1881 when Warren Tay noted some abnormal eye findings in two "Hebrew infants" in London. In 1887, Bernard Sachs provided a more comprehensive clinical and pathological description of the disease, again in children of Eastern European origin. It would be another decade before the disease was identified in a non-Jewish infant. In one extensive study, 104 of 111 kinships were Jewish. Clearly, TSD was a Jewish disease.

However, when pediatricians developed a greater awareness of TSD, it became apparent that many non-Jewish infants were afflicted with it, but that the disease had gone unrecognized. The sensitive awareness of TSD in the Jewish community had not yet spread to the majority population.

The development of a blood test to detect carriers of TSD changed the nationwide perception of this disease. The carrier rate among American Jews was one in 30. In certain clusters it was as high as one in 19, while the carrier rate in American non-Jews was about one in 300. It thus became a nonsectarian disease. Therefore, in a comprehensive national survey undertaken in 1960, there were about 165,000 Jewish carriers and 521,000 non-Jewish carriers of TSD.

With the advent of routine blood testing for the TSD carrier-state, particularly in young Jewish populations, followed by appropriate genetic counseling, most cases of TSD were prevented. At the present time, nationwide, infants born with TSD are largely non-Jewish.

Collective guilt, disease, and the blame game

One of the so-called minor prophets, Jonah, is remembered largely, if not solely, as the victim of the carnivorous tendencies of a great fish.

Yet Jonah's tale, brief and apocryphal as it may be, contains a subtle lesson of far more profound significance than merely a near-fatal maritime encounter with that marine creature. It instructs us also, by a fanciful and deceptively simple metaphor, about the evolution of humans from their earlier status as inseparable parts of a closely integrated tribal society, to a later time when they became identified more as individuals with individual responsibilities.

Jonah is commanded by God to take himself to Nineveh to convey the Lord's message of retribution. Jonah refuses his assignment and instead secretly boards a ship to Tarshish, (a scriptural name for Spain). The vessel encounters a mighty storm, the earthly representation of God's wrath. The many sailors, all nameless, cringe in fright and pray to their respective gods for salvation. All pray but Jonah, who knows the origin of the fateful storm. He refrains from prayers, aware that his secret iniquity has placed the lives of others in jeopardy. The storm persists despite the many urgent prayers to heathen gods. Jonah finally admits his guilt and begs the crew to throw him overboard. With reluctance they cast him into the sea where he is promptly devoured by a huge creature, a leviathan, and the storm immediately abates.

Jonah repents, and after days he is expelled from the creature's stomach, still alive, thus allowing him to reach shore and belatedly fulfill God's demands. Implicit in this allegory is the sense of collective guilt; one man aboard this vessel has sinned, yet all were held to share his guilt, and the entire crew might well have perished were it not for their action in casting Jonah overboard. Nor is this concept of collective guilt a uniquely Semitic notion. One of the great dramas of ancient Greece, *Oedipus Rex* by Sophocles, tells the story of a terrible plague overcoming the city of Thebes because of the hidden guilt of one man, Oedipus. Disease, to the ancients, was a divinely ordained act and a direct response to societal guilt. Even though the taint of sin was confined to the hands of one or two, the entire multitude was remorselessly made to suffer, either through the terrible burden of some awesome infectious disease, as with Thebes, or rapidly through fire and brimstone as with Sodom and Gomorrah.

Over the millennia, disease has been gradually transformed from a divinely ordained collective punishment to a totally secular transaction; and yet remnants of the supernatural origin of sicknesses linger. The days of condemning the entire population of Nineveh, or Sodom or Gomorrah for the bestialities of a few are past, although some remnants still persist.

Consider, for example, a newly arrived highly communicable disease, called cholera, in Providence. Until the early decades of the 19th century it was a disease confined to that portion of India near the Ganges River and the territories neighboring on the Bay of Bengal. The disease was endemic to this region with a frighteningly high mortality rate. It seemed to reach epidemic proportions, especially during the annual religious pilgrimages to the shores of the Ganges and other holy rivers. When British troops entered this region, they too developed cholera, but at far lower frequency and with a lower mortality rate. Then, as the British military units drove deeper into the heartland of India, the disease seemed to follow and take root in regions not previously burdened by cholera. By 1810 the disease had gripped all of India and spread to neighboring nations. By then the Western European nations began to worry as daily reports showed cholera inexorably moving through Russia, Poland and Germany until, finally, by 1817 it had crossed the English Channel to Britain and Scotland. Within weeks it had infiltrated the tenements of London with widespread disease accompanied by panic.

The Americas now began to take notice as the disease emerged in the Quebec Province of Canada, and the poorer neighborhoods of New York. Despite quarantining measures (including the barring of New Yorkers from entering Providence via the Boston Post Road), cholera surfaced in downtown Providence in the late August of 1831. Within weeks the initial two cases were joined by scores of newly infected Rhode Islanders. The nature of the disease was not understood; its treatment was either ineffectual or actually harmful, and certainly its cause was an utter mystery. Thus a frightened community was prompted to speculate.

And speculation surely was rife. Since the great majority of cholera cases were confined to the waterfront inhabitants, sermon after righteous sermon declared that the disease was clearly the hand of God directed specifically against the wicked of the city. Since the waterfront included the city's brothels, saloons and the wretched tenements for newly arrived immigrants from Ireland, these victims of cholera were blamed because of the "errors" of their religion and their alleged consumption of whisky. The sins of the brothels needed no explanation to rapt congregations.

Only later did medicine demonstrate that the germs of cholera propagated in drinking water when it was contaminated with sewage from neighboring cesspools. Cholera turned out to be a gastrointestinal disease of poverty rather than a moral failing. Until that became apparent, entire ethnic groups were condemned.

Jonah's tale describes an entire shipload of humans condemned because of the inadequacies of one man. It is a story which reflects an era when tribal survival depended upon the cooperative efforts of all its members. It was an era, too, when the failings of one person might indeed cause disaster for all of his tribal cohorts. Thus, too, it was a time when inexplicable events such as famine or disease could only be explained away by this individual's failings; thus provoking divine anger.

IQ tests, alleged mental deficiency of Jews, other ethnic groups

Intelligence is one of those words which defies accurate definition. Largely, it describes an individual's aggregate capacity to analyze incoming signals, to act purposefully, sometimes creatively, to think rationally and to deal effectively when confronted with novel situations and challenges.

Psychologists have long believed that intelligence is not some murky quality but rather is an attribute that can be measured and even ranked. The first formal inquiries into intelligence and its measurement (so-called psychometrics) arose with the research efforts of Alfred Binet (1857-1911), professor of psychology at the University of Paris. His early investigations recorded skull measurements, a popular pseudo-science called craniometry which claimed that cranial volume was correlated with intelligence. Binet's diligent studies on the head-measurements of children, however, showed no significant concordancy between skull dimensions and intelligence.

Binet next devised a series of tests of increasing difficulty, to determine the capacity of children to solve problems. Binet's series of tests underwent many revisions until his 1908 version which consisted of a sequence of intellectual challenges, each one appropriate to particular age. Thus, if a child of age 8 could solve problems up to the age 8 test, but no further, his "mental age" was said to be 8.

In 1912 a German psychologist refined this measurement by defining intelligence as the mental age divided by the chronological age, multiplied by 100. And since the resultant number represented the act of dividing one number into another, it was called an intelligence quotient, or IQ. Thus, a child of 8 with a mental age of 8 would be assigned an IQ of 100. Quotients at or near 100 were deemed normal while those significantly below 100 were considered indicative of mentally deficiency.

Binet appreciated that human intelligence was much too complex a phenomenon to be portrayed by a single number the way one might define height or body weight. Accordingly, he used his intelligence quotient scales solely for the purpose of identifying those young children encountering educational difficulties; those who would be helped by a more individually structured education.

He refused to label them as innately deficient in intelligence. Low IQ scores, in his judgment, did not label the child as permanently or congenitally incapable of learning. And certainly the IQ scores should never be used to determine social rank, eligibility (or ineligibility) for any position or profession.

The use of a test allegedly to determine intelligence found a ready and willing audience in England and the United States. H. H. Goddard, an authority in the management of institutions for the mentally deficient (and the inventor of the word "moron"), was a pioneer in the broad application of the IQ test for social and political purposes extending far beyond Binet's visions. Goddard convinced the U.S. Army to use a modified Binet test on all of its conscripts before and during World War I. Goddard segregated the test results according to the ethnic origins of the military inductees. He thus found that certain immigrant groups scored below average (Italians, Jews and non-Jews of Eastern European descent) identifying them as deficient intellectually; while those of northwestern European origin (British, German, Scandinavian) scored above average. He concluded that intelligence was a genetically determined property.

The data, and the conclusions drawn by Goddard, Terman and Yerkes, were happily accepted by Congress when it revised the 1924 Immigration Restriction Act setting quotas on the numbers, per country, entering the United States, and were established by a fear that feeble-minded Italians, Jews and Poles would flood the country and adulterate the earlier ethnic stock that created and sustained this nation. Goddard felt the need to "limit, segregate and curtail breeding" of these and other "lesser" ethnicities.

Carl Brigham, a professor of psychology at Princeton, was more explicit in his assertions. In 1923, he stated that intelligence is largely a genetic phenomenon. And he, too, concluded that the Italians, Russians, Poles and Jews were intellectually inferior to northwest European stock.

In England authorities such as Francis Galton and Karl Pearson declared the undesirability of Jewish immigration into Britain. They worried that Jewish immigrants were "specialized for a parasitical existence." Pearson's research led him to conclude: "… this alien Jewish population is somewhat inferior physically and mentally to the native population." Since he believed that intelligence was an inherited quality, it made sense then to selectively exclude such intellectually inferior groups as the European Jews.

The conclusions and recommendations of Goddard, Brigham and Pearson were uncritically adopted by those in Nazi Germany responsible for the ethnic policies leading to the flawed concepts of racial purity.

The earnest attempts of a French educator, Alfred Binet, to develop a test to identify and then aid academically challenged school children became, in the hands of others, an evil social instrument which denied certain classes of immigrants entrance to England and the United States.

'They grew fat and gross and coarse'

Gluttony, the offense of chronic overeating, was a late entrant to the roster of cardinal sins. For most of human history episodes of drought, famine and starvation were much more in evidence than the rare intervals when there had been an over-abundance of food for the general populace.

On those uncommon occasions when a community was confronted with an excess of food, the people generally rejoiced with binge-eating feasts. But since the means of storing and preserving food had not yet been perfected, these brief interludes of gluttony were typically followed by extended periods of substandard nutrition.

Overeating – and its medical component, obesity – was therefore an isolated phenomenon and typically confined to the wealthy and powerful. As recently as the 19th century, excessive eating was an indulgence entertained by few; and fictional rulers, mercantile leaders and executives were typically portrayed as portly while their workers were pictured as undernourished, even gaunt. Furthermore, corpulent people such as St. Nicholas, Falstaff or Dickens' Mr. Pickwick, were described as benign, generous and outgoing while villainous people such as Simon Legree, Cassius or Richard III were defined as lean, sinister and dangerous. (Caesar declares: "Let me have men about me that are fat, sleek-headed men and such as sleep o'nights; Yon' Cassius has a lean and hungry look; He thinks too much, such men are dangerous.")

Only occasionally do the fat ones of past history indicate that being fat might also be medically hazardous. Shakespeare's Falstaff exclaims: "Thou seest I have more flesh than another man, and therefore more frailty."

How did the Bible view food and obesity? When pharaoh invited Joseph and his family to settle in his kingdom, he declares: "I will give you the good of the land of Egypt, and ye shall eat the fat of the land." Fat as a symbol generally signified comfort, safety, peace and prosperity. Moses' song, (Deuteronomy 32: 1-39) uses food to show God's caring for the People of Israel:

He set him atop the highlands,

To feast on the yield of the earth,
He fed him honey from the crag,
And oil from the flinty rock,
Butter of cow and milk of flocks
With the fat of lambs.

The song continues to describe the times when the Israelites corrupted themselves and gave rise to a perverse and crooked generation. They took on and worshipped alien gods and forsook the Rock of their salvation. They "grew fat and gross and coarse." Thus, at a time in human history when the primary danger to any tribal community rested in starvation, Deuteronomy equated overeating with coarseness, self-indulgence, sloth, apostasy and deep lapses in faith.

Today's physicians know that obesity and overeating are not simple phenomena akin to a spigot which can be turned on or off. Eating, like sex, is one of the sustaining forces of life that are rarely stayed after minimal biological needs are fulfilled. Man is the only animal that eats when he is not hungry, drinks when he is not thirsty and has sex in all seasons regardless of any need for offspring.

Most people identify food as one of the primary pleasures in life. Certainly, beyond its crucial nutritional role, food is central to virtually every religious or secular ritual. Births, commencements, weddings, anniversaries, retirements – even deaths – are each commemorated by a defining meal with certain prescribed foods and libations.

Physicians recognize that obesity has now reached epidemic proportions. And while obesity, in the past, had been a sign of upper class socio-economic status, the reverse now pertains.

For the foreseeable future, eating (and overeating) seems destined to satisfy much more than hunger pangs. Its emotional role, beyond the need for basic sustenance is diverse, complex and tangled. For some, it is a cherished preoccupation, for others an addiction, and for still others an activity intermingled with social imperatives, taboos, religious prohibitions and uncounted swirling and unconscious forces.

The hazards of overeating are enormous in terms of the life-shortening nature of obesity and its companion cardiovascular disease. But, long before the science of clinical nutrition had evolved, it is interesting that the Bible considered overeating as morally repugnant.

Yellow fever: the great American plague

In the early decades of the 19th century, a small wooden building, little more than a rudimentary shack, was erected on a promontory adjacent to Narragansett Bay. Its purpose was to provide quarantine quarters for those on sailing vessels showing the visible signs of a terrible pestilence called yellow fever. This was a disease of puzzling properties. It didn't seem to be contagious yet it spread, much like a contagion, through affected communities. Quarantining in this marine hospital did not diminish the local outbreaks of yellow fever but it served to show a credulous populace that the Rhode Island government was doing something to confront this fearful pestilence.

Yellow fever attacked Rhode Island in the last decade of the 18th century. But other than the local epidemic of 1797, the state escaped the major yellow fever devastations experienced by cities such as Philadelphia (in 1793), Memphis (in 1878) and New Orleans (in 1903). To understand the manner by which yellow fever spreads from one victim to another, it is necessary to review its mortal path through recent human history, beginning with the rampant colonialism initiated by European nations in the 16th century.

In his journal for the year 1648, the Spanish archivist, Lopez de Cogolludo, recorded a terrible pestilence in the Mexican Yucatan peninsula. He described the malady as beginning with intense headache, muscle pains, raging fever and, what made the illness so distinguishable, the emergence of a yellow tint to the skin and eyeballs of the victim. Death was a common outcome. He noted, particularly in fatal cases, that the victim also developed persistent vomiting (with the vomitus looking like coffee-grounds). In latter years the disease became known as *fiebre marillo, fievre jaune*, yellow fever or simply yellow jack.

The Spanish presumed that it was a local pestilence confined to the Caribbean islands and neighboring Mexico although the Portuguese had independently encountered the illness in their newly established colonies on the Brazilian coast. The mortality rate amongst both European colonials and indigenous Native Americans was tragically high but less so in slaves of African origin. The disease festered during the next century but was considered to be, like other alleged Caribbean sicknesses, a reasonable price to be paid for colonial exploitation.

In 1778, there was an outbreak of yellow fever in British troops stationed in Senegal, Africa. And the epidemiological question then emerged: Did yellow fever arise first in the Western Hemisphere or, alternatively, in Africa; or, independently, in both? The question remained unanswered until 18th-century explorers colonizing the upper Niger River noted areas of endemic yellow fever in villages bordering upon the rain forests of the African interior. The disease was particularly prevalent in male workers cutting down trees in response to a European craving for lumber. Yellow fever, amongst the native Africans, however, tended to be mild with a low mortality rate.

The Caribbean islands were progressively colonized by Europeans, particularly from Spain, England and France, during the beginning decades of the 18th century; and yellow fever, accordingly, became transformed from isolated outbreaks to a devastating disease of epidemic proportions changing the course of Western Hemispheric history. The Caribbean plantation workers, originally derived from the European (particularly English) unemployed, were decimated by the disease; and history has ascribed two monumental effects of Caribbean yellow fever: First, it became the major stimulus for the slave trade, from Africa, to replace the Europeans sickened by yellow fever, since it was believed that Africans were partially immune to the disease; and second, it encouraged France to abandon its plans for an income-producing colony in Haiti (and later, to forgo its plans, also, for a French empire in North America by selling the Louisiana Territory to the United States in 1803).

The 19th century saw no lessening of the mortal effects of yellow fever, particularly on the Caribbean islands. And while it assumed the dubious role of becoming the Great American Plague, curiously, it never spread to the great population centers of Asia.

The United States witnessed three major yellow fever epidemics. The first paralyzed Philadelphia in 1793, then the young nation's capitol. The fever had been brought to the Delaware River region by refugee plantation owners and their families, fleeing the revolution in Haiti.

The island of Cuba, a Spanish possession, became the endemic center of yellow fever in the 19th century; and represented a major public health problem to the invading American armies in the Spanish-

American War commencing in 1898. It was the need to lessen the burden of yellow fever, both upon the American military in Cuba and the American workforce in Panama (where they were trying to construct an inter-ocean canal) that finally led to a solution to how yellow fever was transmitted from one human to another; and how, by having this precious information, the disease might ultimately be contained.

Yellow fever: An imported pestilence

Of the many pestilences that have burdened the nations of the Western Hemisphere, one stands out as uniquely American despite the paradox that it originated in the rain forests of western Africa where it was quietly endemic and represented only a negligible public health threat. But then it was brought to the West by the 16th-century slave ships. Yellow fever, sometimes called the American Plague, was thus newly established in the Caribbean islands and the mainland of the Americas. By the 17th century it exhibited a substantially higher mortality rate, ravaging the mainland of both western continents, particularly the densely populated port cities such as Charleston and New Orleans. The scourge continued unabated until the early 20th century when, finally, effective sanitarian measures and vaccines were introduced. Yellow fever, small pox, measles and malaria were unknown in the Americas until colonization from Europe changed the demography and disease profile of the Western Hemisphere.

The cause as well as the mechanism by which yellow fever was transferred from one person to the next remained a mystery until 1881 when Carlos J. Finlay, a practicing physician in Havana, proposed the outlandish notion that the disease was transmitted by the bite of a female mosquito that had been infected by having previously bitten a human in the active stages of yellow fever.

The role of insects as propagating agents – as vectors – in the spread of infectious disease had been uniformly deemed preposterous; after all, how could a barely visible, frail bug cause a 200-pound adult to become mortally ill ? But in 1878, a Scottish physician named Patrick Manson, working in the Far East, demonstrated that a particular species of mosquito spread a tropical disease of humans called filariasis. In 1893, the American scientist, Theobald Smith, showed that the tick was responsible for the spread of a bacterial disease of cattle and latter, the mechanism by which Rocky Mountain spotted fever was propagated. And yet another Scottish physician, Ronald Ross, in 1897, showed that female mosquitoes of the *Anopheles* genus caused the transmission of malaria. The proposals put forth by Finlay found little initial support in the medical community; and his unfunded attempts to experimentally reproduce the disease failed.

A decade later, an American commission, headed by Maj. Walter Reed, undertook more structured experiments to elucidate how yellow fever was spread. Following Finlay's suggestion, they were able to demonstrate, in 1898, that infected mosquitoes of the species *Aedes egyptii* could indeed infect human "volunteers." Reed's colleagues additionally demonstrated that the infective agent was smaller than a bacterium and hence in a class of pathogens called viruses; and further, that the effectiveness of the mosquito vector was climatologically restricted since the *Aedes* species do not function in temperatures lower than 60 degrees. Epidemiologists noted that the peak frequencies of the insect-borne (such as malaria or yellow fever) coincided with the time of year when the responsible insects were most active.

Further studies of the biological characteristics of the *Aedes* strains of mosquito revealed that they propagated readily in puddles of stagnant water, in discarded receptacles and even in shallow, rain-filled ruts in plowed fields. Knowing how and where these mosquitoes thrived, and what their biological limitations were, then allowed Army engineers to plan an extensive campaign in Cuba to rid the island of sites of mosquito proliferation. Thus, without any specific therapy against yellow fever, the Army sanitarians were able to reduce the frequency of yellow fever to manageable levels. Furthermore, using the same anti-mosquito measures, the construction of the Panama Canal could then proceed without the peril of yellow fever epidemics that had caused the French to abandon their earlier attempts at canal construction in Panama.

The tragic history of yellow fever might be considered complete when Dr. Max Theiler developed an effective and safe vaccine, in 1933. This, in association with effective pesticide campaigns and the widespread use of window screening, has virtually eliminated the disease from the Western Hemisphere. The year 1905 saw the last case of yellow fever in the United States. The typical American physician has never encountered a case of yellow fever. But it would be negligent if it was not also recalled that yellow fever would not have been established in the Western Hemisphere, causing millions of deaths, were it not for the evil practice of enslaving native Africans and bringing them to this half of the globe. The slave ships carried active victims of the disease as well as the transmitting mosquitoes. And once established in the Caribbean basin, both the disease and the transmitting insects multiplied.

It should be remembered, too, that yellow fever (and some of the other plagues transported by the process of colonization and slavery) served to kill most of the native population of the Americas who were immunologically unprepared for this alien virus. In the sober words of the historian, Noble D. Cook, "The century and a half after 1492 witnessed, in terms of the number of people who died, the greatest human catastrophe in history, far exceeding even the disaster of the Black Death of medieval Europe."

Ellis Island: Isle of Hope and Dreams

By Brown Brothers, ca. 1908

Immigrant children, Ellis Island, New York. Vintage print. *Records of the Public Health Service.* **(90-G-125-29).**

'For I am a stranger amidst thee'*

There is something magical about islands that transform themselves into sanctuaries that are mysterious yet memorable. Many of these pieces of real estate are romantic places such as Bermuda, Capri (*Isola d'Amore*), Oahu, Crete and Aruba. But there is one island with neither beaches nor gardens nor anything esthetically noteworthy, yet is an island etched into the memories of over 100 million Americans.

This particular island began life as a rocky shoal, barely inches above the tidal waters of upper New York Harbor. The Dutch called these three acres Oyster Island because of its abundance of shellfish. Samuel Ellis bought the islet in 1785 but then sold it to the United States Army as a site for the safe storage of munitions. The islet was then selected by the government in 1890 as its newly empowered Immigration and Naturalization Service (INS) site. The islet was inadequate to fulfill the spatial needs of the INS; and so untold tons of rock and soil, excavated from Manhattan as the underground subways were being constructed, were added to enlarge the island to a utilitarian rectangle housing the immigration facilities as well as public health hospitals and holding areas for those immigrants considered for deportation.

On Jan. 1, 1892, the facility began the task of processing the flood of immigrants traveling from Europe. Ellis Island represented but one of many immigration depots established on the East Coast. Others stations included those in Baltimore, Philadelphia, Boston – and even Providence.

Before Ellis Island became functional, immigrants were processed at the lower end of Manhattan Island, in what is now Castle Clinton in Battery Park. The building began life in 1811 as a fort to protect New York from the marauding British; then it was recast as a somewhat shady dance and beer hall; and then altered again to process immigrants and eventually named Castle Clinton (after the 19th-century governor of New York.) This site was finally abandoned because of a variety of logistic problems.

The numbers passing through the INS facility in New York harbor were truly immense. By November of 1954, when the INS station on

Ellis Island was closed, after 62 years of uninterrupted service, over 12 million souls were processed. And this did not include an additional four million immigrants who, as first- or second-class passengers on the liners, could bypass Ellis Island and be subjected to but a cursory examination by the INS inspectors who boarded the liners

The following conditions — either medical, cognitive, ethnic or socio-political – were grounds for excluding newly arrived immigrants. Amongst medical conditions were: tuberculosis, leprosy, venereal disease, goiter, hernias, trachoma, epilepsy, physical deformities, "loathsome or contagious diseases," or pregnancy in a woman unaccompanied by a husband. Cognitive factors included mental deficiency, inexplicable demeanor, manic or immoral behavior and, after 1917, illiteracy. Socio-political factors included past criminal behavior, polygamy or membership in political organizations such as the communist or anarchist parties. Ethnic barriers to admission, particularly on the West Coast, included Chinese aliens (as specified in the Chinese Exclusion Act of 1882).

How many have been excluded for medical reasons? In a typical year, with about 800,000 immigrants entering Ellis Island (called by many the "Palace of Hope, the Island of Tears"), about 17,000 (1 in 43), were sent back to Europe largely because of tuberculosis, mental deficiency or trachoma. In the 62-year history of Ellis Island, 610,000 were excluded.

By 1922, when regional quotas for admission were established, vast numbers of immigrants had been admitted to these shores including 4.6 million Irish, 5.9 million Germans, 4.7 million Italians, 4.1 million from Austro-Hungary, 3.4 million from Great Britain, 3.3 million Russians (including Poles, Ukrainians and Lithuanians), and 1.2 million Swedes. Jews immigrating to this nation were not listed separately but were subsumed under those numbers originating in Russia, Austro-Hungary and Germany. An estimated 2.7 million Jews passed through the Island.

Jewish immigrants

What distinguished these Jewish immigrants? Certainly no difference in the degree of poverty. But the Jews tended to arrive in families rather than as isolated, unmarried young people; and further, they were met by groups such as the Hebrew Immigrant Aid Society

(HIAS), to aid them in seeking immediate shelter and a stable setting to begin their lives in the *Goldene Medina*.

Amongst those passing through Ellis Island were the following Jews: David Dubinsky, Emma Goldman, Hyman Rickover, Abe Beame, Samuel Goldwyn, Al Jolson, Irving Berlin, Isaac Asimov, Henry Roth, Lee Strasberg, Victor Borge, Sol Hurok, Max Factor, Edward G. Robinson – and even Meyer Lansky.

Jews had some past experience in voyaging to new communities. Moses, who led the Israelites through alien territory, had a son born to Zipporah; he was called Gershom, because his name meant "I have been a stranger in a strange land." (Exod. 2:22). And later the Lord instructed Moses saying: "But a stranger that dwelleth with you shall be unto you as one born among you and thou shall love him as thyself; for you were strangers in Egypt." (Levit.19:34).

*: Psalm 39.

Chapter 6

The man who created medicines out of the earth

It was the year of 1888 and Alexander III, Tsar of all the Russias, ruled a sprawling empire which embraced the wilderness of the steppes, great cities such as St. Petersburg and the anonymous *shtetls* of the Western Pale. In one such small village on the plains of Ukraine, Priluka by name, a son was born to Fradia and Jacob Waksman. With great prescience they named him after Solon the wise, a name which was later translated to English as Selman.

> *He sought for a word which might describe the phenomenon whereby some microorganisms inhibit the growth of others. Finding no such word, he invented one: antibiotic.*

At an early age, Selman showed great intellectual skills and his family recruited tutors to augment his customary secular and Talmudic education. But the doors to Russia's great universities were denied to him. His family then located a distant friend, Professor Jacob Lipman at Rutgers University, New Jersey, to aid young Selman in his quest for an education in the sciences. Lipman had already established an enviable record as an outstanding soil scientist. He obtained a scholarship for Selman, and four years later, in 1915, Waksman received his baccalaureate degree from Rutgers with highest honors; a year later came the master's degree in soil sciences, and in 1918, a doctorate in biochemistry from the University of California.

Selman then returned to the New Jersey Agricultural Experiment Station, a branch of Rutgers, to begin a research and teaching career, during the next four decades, in the relatively unexplored domain of the bacteria and other microscopic organisms populating the soil and sea water. It was an arcane field of study which did not cross the consciousness of the average American. The soil microbiologist was not exactly a profession to quicken the pulse or enter into the febrile dreams of ambitious young students seeking a profession. A diligent student of life within soil, Waksman brought order out of chaos.

In the next decade, Waksman established himself as a diligent student of all forms of microscopic life within the soil. He demonstrated the vast and diversified population of bacteria, viruses, fungi and protozoa within the earth. Gradually, though, his research narrowed itself to the poorly understood soil fungi. Waksman changed a chaotic field to one with a rational system of classification based largely upon the most modern principles of biochemistry. He and his many graduate students isolated countless new species, studied their role in the complex interrelationships within soil and began to seek an understanding of the environmental circumstances which either inhibited or encouraged their growth.

In these early years, Waksman also undertook research into the chemical reactions within compost, humus and peat, to agronomists attempting to develop more rational means of crop development and soil fertilization.

The Actinomyces, a genus of fungus first identified in 1875, became the object of his intense study. Inevitably these studies led to a curiosity regarding the unstable balances between microbial coexistence and antagonism. He recognized that the struggle for life, so obvious in the jungle, exists in soil with the same intensity. And he began to appreciate the complexity of this struggle for survival. He sought for a word which might describe the phenomenon whereby some microorganisms inhibit the growth of others. Finding no such word, he invented one: antibiotic. He defined it as "a chemical substance, produced by microorganisms, which has the capacity to inhibit the growth and even to destroy bacteria and other organisms in dilute solutions."

In confronting all of these biochemical intricacies, he wondered whether the ceaseless, competitive interrelationship within soil might somehow yield benefits for mankind. In 1932, for example, he was struck by the chance observation that the mycobacteria – the germs

140

that cause human tuberculosis – would not survive when intermixed with soil.

He noted further that the growth of many forms of soil bacteria was stunted when grown with the actinomyces but not by the exhaustion of those nutrients necessary for bacterial growth. This led him to the inevitable conclusion that some substance must be elaborated by the fungi which was in some manner destructive to the adjacent bacteria. He finally isolated and concentrated this substance—calling it actinomycin—and was astonished to observe that a very small amount, in a test tube, destroyed vast numbers of certain bacteria.

Actinomycin, unfortunately, proved to be quite toxic to mammals and an intensive search was then begun to isolate other antibiotic producing fungi. In 1943, a species of Streptomyces (*S. griseus*) was isolated in Waksman's laboratory. By January of 1944 an antibiotic substance was found in the cultures of this organism, a substance called streptomycin. By 1945 it was shown to be effective against the bacteria causing tuberculosis, and for the first time in history, the medical profession possessed a therapeutic weapon to fight the great white plague of consumption.

In the next decade, Waksman's laboratory isolated a succession of antibiotics from various species of fungi. Truly, in the Scriptural words chosen by one of Waksman's co-workers: "The Lord hath created medicines out of the earth."

In 1952, the Nobel Prize in medicine was awarded to Professor Selman Waksman for his monumental contributions to the field of antibiotic therapies. In but 64 years, less than a lifetime, he had risen from a Yiddish-speaking *shtetl* in the Ukraine to the majestic community of the Nobel laureates.

The man who invented vitamins

The naming of a newborn child is a serious undertaking. When doing so parents are customarily influenced by many considerations: family names from the past, religious traditions, even secular fashions. Jewish families, if assimilated into the majority middle class, may select a name with no connection to their ethnic heritage, a name perhaps of some national leader. But even here certain sensitivities generally prevail; few 19th century Russian-Jewish families, for example, named their sons after the ruling tsars. In Poland, though, the name of Casimir, dead some six centuries, was still honored by the Jews. King Casimir III (1310-1370), at least by 14th-century standards, was unusually benevolent to the Jews, encouraging them to emigrate to his largely agrarian kingdom.

In seeking a name for his creation, this wondrous micronutrient, Funk reached into traditional scientific lexicon and combined the Latin word for life (vita) and the chemical structure of his isolate (an amine), thus coining the word "vitamine."

In 1884, in Warsaw, a third son was born to Jacob and Gustawa Funk. (Two prior sons had died in childhood.) The father was a respected physician specializing in dermatology; the mother was an educated woman much involved in the cultural life of her city. They named their offspring Casimir.

Casimir's parents surrounded him with an abundance of protective care and affection. Sadly, he was afflicted with a congenital dislocation of his hip and despite frequent consultations throughout Europe and numerous surgical interventions the impairment forced the child to spend his early childhood at home.

Casimir's education was personally supervised by his parents; by age eight he was fluent in eight languages and conversant with the works of many European authors, particularly Dickens, Dumas and Verne.

Before the age of 10, he had absorbed the works of Darwin, Huxley and other 19th-century scientists.

At age 16, Casimir left Poland to begin his collegiate education, first in Geneva and later in Berne. He concentrated his studies initially in botany but switched to the relatively new field of biochemistry in the belief that this scientific discipline possessed more potential. He was awarded his doctoral degree in 1904.

The Pasteur Institute in Paris beckoned and for the next three years Funk worked as a research assistant to Professor Gabriel Bertrand. After the decorous atmosphere of bourgeois Berne, Paris was a revelation, a dazzling world beyond the laboratory and library. Funk discovered the theater, with the immortal Bernhardt, and the sidewalk cafes where philosophic inquiry mixed comfortably with spirits, the ardor of politics and the passions of interpersonal relationships.

In 1906, Funk transferred to Berlin, then the center of biochemical research. He missed the pleasures of Paris but now had the opportunity to work under Emil Fischer, Germany's leading organic chemist. In 1910, a research position providing a measure of autonomy opened in the Lister Institute and Funk, now married and soon to be a father, transferred to London.

At about this time a Dutch scientist named Eijkmann had demonstrated that chickens fed exclusively with polished rice (i.e., rice grains deprived of their husks) developed a progressive loss of peripheral nerve function quite similar to the human disease called beriberi. Eijkmann had speculated that husked rice grain harbored a toxic substance causing nerve damage and that the husks contained a neutralizing antitoxin.

The problem intrigued Funk, who embarked upon a series of experiments which ultimately provided an answer to the enigmas of beriberi. In retrospect, his findings did much more – they envisioned a new category of human disease.

Funk began his laboratory inquiries by asking the fundamental question that any research chemist might ask: What is the biochemical structure of the substance which prevents, or cures, experimental beriberi, regardless of whether it functions as an antitoxin, as an essential protein component or in some other as yet unrecognized manner? His first task then, as he saw it, was to isolate the putative anti-beriberi substance.

Using a variety of analytic procedures, he reduced tons of rice huskings to various fractions, testing each for its potency in preventing experimental beriberi. After repeated fractionation he was left with a nitrogenous substance which, in exceedingly minute amounts, prevented beriberi.

In seeking a name for his creation, this wondrous micronutrient, Funk reached into traditional scientific lexicon and combined the Latin word for life (*vita*) and the chemical structure of his isolate (an *amine*), thus coining the word "vitamine." And in a summary paper he then proposed the novel thought that there was a family of clinical disorders not caused by germs, poisons, or physical injuries but by a deficiency of these dietary chemicals - called vitamins (the 'e' in vitamines was dropped by 1920). He suggested that beriberi, pellagra, rickets and scurvy would fall within the scope of this disease-category.

For the next four decades Funk continued his labors on the biochemistry of nutrition, playing a major role in determining the chemical structure of such vital substances as niacin (dietary deficiency of which causes pellagra). Much of his work was accomplished in the United States although shortly after the end of World War II he returned to Warsaw where, for a few years, he established and directed a nutritional institute funded by the Rockefeller Foundation.

Funk's immense contribution to medicine, aside from the distinction of coining the word vitamin, was his innovative concept that certain chemicals - beyond the major macronutrients (fats, proteins and carbohydrates) - fulfilled an essential role in the metabolic reactions of the human body; and that certain specific diseases may arise when any one of these micronutrients, called vitamins, was lacking in the diet.

Three very determined women who won the Nobel Prize

W hen Alfred Bernhard Nobel died in 1896, his will stipulated that a generous gift, a prize, be awarded annually to those who had contributed materially to the fields of peace, literature, chemistry, physics, and physiology and medicine.

The first woman to be awarded this prestigious prize was Marie S. Curie, in 1905, for her studies in the physics of radioactivity. Since this inaugural award, other women have been similarly recognized: one receiving the prize in physics, three in chemistry, 10 in peace, nine in literature and six in physiology and medicine.

One pursued her scientific inquiries in a remote Italian farmhouse; another worked as a quality-control chemist for a food company, and the third was employed as a junior technician in a Veteran's hospital in the Bronx.

The lives of the six women honored in medicine and physiology (Cori in 1947, Yalow in 1977, McClintock in 1983, Levi-Montalcini in 1986, Elion in 1988, and Nusslein-Volhard in 1995) are chronicles of courage, tenacity and sheer brilliance. All were required to struggle in male- dominated professions often with meager research facilities. Few had protective mentors or enduring financial backing in their investigative pursuits, and three of the six were Jewish.

Rita Levi-Montalcini was born in Turin, Italy on April 22, 1909, the youngest of four children. Her father was Adamo Levi, a mathematician and electrical engineer; her mother was the celebrated painter, Adele Montalcini. She grew to maturity in a highly cultured home where the arts and intellectual activates were encouraged. Rita and her two sisters, however, were dissuaded from attending college. Rita persisted, educating herself in the classical languages, and at age 20 entered the University's medical school. Two of her medical school classmates, Salvador Luria and Renato Dulbecco, were later to immigrate to the United States, and the three, in unrelated fields of fundamental biological research, were recipients of the Nobel Prize.

Levi-Montalcini was awarded her medical degree in 1936, intent upon a career in neurology. But 1936 saw the enactment of fascist Italy's racial laws which forbade academic careers for non-Aryans. Levi-Montalcini fled to Belgium but returned to Turin in 1940 to avoid the invading German armies. With neither an exit visa nor a place to work, Levi-Montalcini elected to convert her bedroom into a research laboratory and animal room. There, for the next three years she pursued investigations concerning the chemical basis of nervous system maturation using mice that she bred beneath her bed. By 1943, she was forced to abandon her small laboratory, fleeing south to join the underground partisans in Florence. In August of 1944, elements of the American army entered Florence and Levi-Montalcini was recruited as a physician to manage the refugee camps, at the time the site of terrible epidemics of typhus fever.

In 1947, she was invited to continue her neurobiologic research at Washington University in St. Louis in collaboration with Professor Victor Hamburger, whose 1930 research on embryologic development of organs had prompted her home-based studies in Turin. She remained in America for a decade, further defining the details of chemical organizations of cellular growth. She returned to Rome to assume the position of director of the Institute of Cell Biology.

Levi-Montalcini had discovered a protein molecule, called Nerve Growth Factor (NGF), which was essential in the directional growth and differentiation of brain cells. Similar molecules were then shown to be of critical importance in other forms of cell growth, including the spread of tumors. A new and immensely productive field in neuroimmunobiology was thus opened. Professor Levi-Montalcini was awarded the Nobel Prize in 1986.

Gertrude Belle Elion, a first-generation American, was born in New York City on Jan. 23, 1918. Her parents had fled the *shtetls* of Eastern Europe. Her intellectual skills were recognized at an early age and she was permitted to attend college at age 15. In 1938 Hunter College (then the sister-school of City College of New York) awarded her a baccalaureate degree. She then took graduate courses in chemistry at

New York University, earning a master's degree in 1941. She experienced difficulty finding employment, finally working in various food packaging concerns. Her interests in pharmacological chemistry finally caught the attention of the Wellcome Research Laboratories in North Carolina and she began a laboratory in collaboration with Dr. George Hitchings, a scientific partnership which lasted for almost four decades.

Elion's research was based on the premise that nucleic acid metabolism was crucial to all growing cells. Her goal, in her words, ". . . was to select specific organisms that we wanted to get rid of and target them in this manner without hurting the host." By 1945 Elion and Hitchings demonstrated vast differences in nucleic acid metabolism in normal cells, cancer cells, and even bacteria. They then devised drugs which selectively interrupted the DNA synthesis within unwanted cells: drugs such as azathioprine for the treatment of gout; acyclovir for the treatment of herpes simplex virus, and trimethoprim for the treatment of bacterial urinary tract infections. In 1969 Brown University recognized Elion's unique scientific breakthroughs and bestowed upon her an honorary doctorate degree. And in 1988, she was awarded the Nobel Prize in Physiology and Medicine.

Rosalyn Sussman Yalow was born in New York City, the daughter of recent immigrants from Eastern Europe. She attended public schools and was admitted to Hunter College, where she trained as a physicist, receiving her bachelor's degree in 1941. She then traveled west where she entered the University of Illinois for graduate studies, culminating in a Ph.D. in 1945. She married a fellow scientist named Yalow.

Finding employment was difficult, but she finally located a civil service job as an assistant physicist at the Veterans Administration Hospital in the Bronx. This location, removed from the great centers of fundamental research, remained her place of work for the next four decades. In conjunction with Dr. Sol Berson, Rosalyn Yalow used newly devised radio-isotopic procedures to investigate the properties of the peptide hormones of the body such as insulin. She invented a technique, called radio-immunoassay, to quantitate incredibly small amounts of circulating hormones, thus opening up a new era in the understanding of endocrine diseases such as diabetes and abnormal thyroid states.

Dr. Yalow had lectured at The Miriam Hospital on many occasions. She takes pride, not only in her laboratory but also its small adjunct kitchen, where for decades she has been preparing kosher meals for her many graduate students. In 1977, the Nobel Prize in Medicine and Physiology was awarded to Rosalyn Sussman Yalow.

Three Jewish women - one from northern Italy, one from Brooklyn and one from the Bronx - separately sought careers in investigative medicine. They encountered immense obstacles in getting educated, in finding appropriate positions and particularly in acquiring suitable laboratory space to pursue their interests. One pursued her scientific inquiries in a remote Italian farmhouse; another worked as a quality-control chemist for a food company, and the third was employed as a junior technician in a Veteran's hospital in the Bronx. But through innate genius, abetted by tenacity and enabling vision, each has made material contributions to the field of fundamental biomedical science and along the way each has been awarded the Nobel Prize.

Abraham Jacobi: The rebel who revolutionized children's medicine

The sorely distressed Israelites struggling in the wilderness of Shur encountered many problems, not the least of which were famine and disease, but the Lord consoled them, saying: "I will not bring upon you any of the diseases that I brought upon the Egyptians, for I the Lord am your healer." And later, when these Israelites were confronted with hostile tribes, they were told, "I will remove sickness from your midst."

Thus the Torah establishes the Lord as undisputed physician to His chosen. There are, of course, numerous preventive interventions to be taken by the mortal Israelites against disease, but nowhere is there mention of any role for secular physicians. And certainly to physicians expressly trained in the treatment of ailing children.

> *"Summoned at the last minute to some emergency case, his entrance was usually dramatic. Dressed in a black overcoat with a flowing black cape, and a broad-rimmed black hat, he would dash up in a black coach drawn by two black horses."*

While the 18th century witnessed the publication of a few tests enumerating ailments of children, the novel idea of a separate clinical discipline confining itself to disorders of the early years of life did not materialize until the mid 19th century. Even the word "paediatrics" (as it was originally spelled), was not encountered before the 1880s.

Historians trace the formal origins of that branch of clinical medicine now called pediatrics to a charismatic German physician named Abraham Jacobi. His youthful years, filled with political turmoil, provided few hints of his later professional accomplishments. Jacobi was born in German Westphalia in 1830, the son of poverty-stricken Jews. His early university studies at Greiswald and Göttingen were concentrated upon Oriental languages, but by age 18, he had transferred to the university in Bonn to prepare himself for a career in medicine.

In concert with many activist collegians, Jacobi participated in the 1848 Revolution which swept through Western Europe. Although acquitted of high treason, he nonetheless languished in a Cologne prison for 18 months before escaping to the port city of Hamburg, where he secured passage to England. From England he sailed to Boston and eventually established himself in New York City as a general practitioner for the small German-Jewish population of Manhattan.

The practice went well, which permitted Jacobi to specialize increasingly in the ill-defined specialty of childhood diseases. By 1860 his skills in treating children were so established that the New York Medical College established for him a chair in childhood diseases, probably the first such academic post to be assigned to the specialty of pediatrics. Within a decade, the more prestigious College of Physicians and Surgeons conferred upon him the professorship of pediatrics, a post that he maintained for 32 years.

During this interval he established at Mt. Sinai Hospital the first pediatric dispensary in the United States and chose a young doctor named Mary Putnam (later to become his wife) as its first director. Jacobi's fame as a consultant in illnesses of childhood spread and he became widely known as "the professor from uptown." One historian described Jacobi's role in consulting within the crowded tenements of the Lower East Side as follows: "Summoned at the last minute to some emergency case, his entrance was usually dramatic. Dressed in a black overcoat with a flowing black cape, and a broad-rimmed black hat, he would dash up in a black coach drawn by two black horses."

Jacobi's association with Mt. Sinai Hospital extended through most of his productive professional career. During the final decades of the 19th century, Jacobi was regarded as this country's leading pediatrician. Indeed, many texts refer to him as the father of academic pediatrics. At this time, he held the presidencies of the American Pediatric Society and the American Medical Association.

During Jacobi's tenure as chief of pediatrics at Mt. Sinai, there gathered under his supervision some of the nation's finest practitioners in diseases of infancy and childhood, among them Dr. Henry Koplik (describer of the Koplik spots in measles), Dr. Bernard Sachs (of Tay-Sachs Disease) and, as his successor, Dr. Bela Schick (of the Schick Test for diphtheria).

When in 1904, Mt. Sinai Hospital moved to its present location on Fifth Avenue and East 100th St., a sumptuous children's pavilion, separate from the other buildings, was included. Its windows looked out upon Central Park and its roof was given over to a spacious nursery solarium. Even classrooms, with public school teachers, were included for those youngsters with chronic ailments. And, of course, there were special bedrooms set aside for parents to stay when their child's medical condition was desperate.

At the cornerstone ceremonies for the new hospital complex, attended by many governmental dignitaries, Abraham Jacobi, now president of the hospital's medical board, was called upon to speak. Reporters described him as a striking figure. "His statuesque head, its gray hair as profuse as ever, suggesting the lion that he was. His reputation for integrity as a doctor and as a fighter for improved medical standards had placed him in the leadership of the New York medical world."

Jacobi's speech that May day described his vision of what role a hospital should fulfill in the new world of the emerging 20th century. He spoke first of the core responsibilities of the hospital in relieving pain, in shortening and preventing disease and in allowing working people to resume their roles as independent wage earners. But the bulk of his speech explored a revolutionary role for the community hospital, that of an education center. "A hospital is a school for doctors who learn and profit in the interest of mankind from collected and collective experience. It is a school for nurses whose very existence was not dreamed of 27 years ago. It is a school for the patients and their families to learn preventive and curative measures. Finally, it is a school for the medical world abroad through the scientific contributions emanating from the institutions."

Jacobi's scientific contributions, particularly in the elucidation of diphtheria and dysentery were immense, as was his campaign to provide free milk for poor children via the Straus Program of milk depots. But his fame will most endure because of his determination to establish a special branch of medicine, now called pediatrics, in behalf of ailing children.

Jacobi, revolutionist and advocate for those who could not speak for themselves, died in the 90th year of his productive life. And when the City of New York, some three decades later, constructed a great municipal teaching hospital adjacent to the new Albert Einstein School of Medicine, they called it the Abraham Jacobi Hospital.

Photo: R.I. Jewish Historical Assn.

Dr. Irving Beck

Irving Beck: The scholar-physician from Providence

Rhode Island is a state of modest size; yet in this last century it has produced more than its share of illustrious physicians. Consider, for example, the career and contributions of native-born Irving Beck.

Irving Addison Beck was born in Providence on Nov. 4, 1911. He attended the local public schools and entered Brown University in 1928. His

> *Yet another field substantially removed from medicine was Beck's abiding interest in the life and literary works of James Joyce.*

undergraduate activities included active participation in the debating union, an academic concentration in biology and election to Phi Beta Kappa.

Following graduation, he attended Harvard Medical School, where his outstanding scholarly achievements earned him the highest of academic honors and led to the esteemed internship and residency in internal medicine at Mt. Sinai Hospital in New York City. He completed his residence training in the perilous year of 1939, just months before the onset of World War II.

Beck returned to his home community of Providence where he established a thriving practice. In 1942, he volunteered for the U.S. Army and was commissioned as captain in the medical corps assigned to chief of laboratory services in the 48th Evacuation Hospital (Rhode Island Hospital unit). The Evacuation Hospital went through the customary stateside orientation and indoctrination in military matters and was then shipped off to eastern India, there to serve as a major base hospital in the China-Burma-India Theater of Operations. Beck employed his three years in India and northern Burma effectively, organizing innovative diagnostic services and sharing his technical experiences in the form of excellent papers for U.S. medical journals.

During this overseas interval he also served on a special armed forces commission exploring the intractable problems of malaria. Upon the completion of the war, Beck, now a major, returned to the States and served briefly as deputy chief of medical services at Camp Edwards in neighboring Massachusetts.

During the 20 years that followed his honorable discharge from the U.S. Army, Beck built an enviable medical practice in Providence and was widely sought as a consultant in internal medicine. By 1962, he had been selected as chief of the medical service at The Miriam and Providence Lying-In Hospitals as well as consultant in internal medicine to Rhode Island and Roger Williams Hospitals.

Brown University, Beck's alma mater, began a master's degree program in biomedicine in 1962 and Beck was chosen as one of the first clinical faculty to counsel these students. In those years of intensely active private practice, Beck also served as president of the Providence Medical Association, governor (for Rhode Island) of the American College of Physicians, president of the Rhode Island Diabetes Association, and president of the prestigious American Osler Society.

Lest the impression be left that Beck's skills were confined to the art and science of medicine, it should be pointed out that he was also regarded as one of the state's leading scholars in book-lore and medical history. Indeed, for decades, he taught a Brown University course, with Professor G. E. Erikson, on medical history. Furthermore, he chaired the State Medical Society's committee on library services and served on the board of trustees of the libraries of Brown University and Harvard Medical School.

Yet another field substantially removed from medicine was Beck's abiding interest in the life and literary works of James Joyce. Indeed, there are many in the greater Providence community who will remember with pleasure Beck's many publications and seminars on the medical odyssey of Joyce.

With the arrival of Brown's accredited medical school in the autumn of 1972, Beck's role in bedside teaching increased. Many of Brown's medical graduates recall those Socratic intervals, typically in the corridors of The Miriam Hospital, when they were allowed to absorb precious fragments from Beck's immense store of clinical insights. His stature as the consummate clinician, in these early years of the medical school, was unique. And Brown was not oblivious to his accomplishments. When the WW Keane Award was established, representing the highest honor which Brown's medical school might confer, Irving Beck was one of the first to be cited "for distinguished achievements and service to the community and to Brown University."

Upon his retirement from the private practice of medicine in 1980, Beck embarked upon a new career. He was chosen as the senior medical consultant to the state-managed hospitals (Rhode Island Medical Center) and for the next decade he undertook to establish a commendable program in the medical education for the staff clinicians, a program which attracted many outside physicians to his excellent weekly seminars in clinical medicine.

Photo: R.I. Jewish Historical Assn.

Dr. Seebert Goldowsky

Seebert Goldowsky, M.D.: A Yankee surgeon

Rhode Island has lost a gifted surgeon, an historian with rare writing skills and an archivist of the Jewish community. Seebert J. Goldowsky, M.D., died on Nov. 3, 1997, in the 90th year of his varied and productive life.

Seebert was born in Providence, the son of a professional detective, said to be the first Jewish private investigator in southern New England. The year of Seebert's birth was 1907. Theodore Roosevelt was president and the Panama Canal would not be opened for another five years.

Seebert attended Classical High School, graduating with virtually all of the scholastic honors available to its seniors. He amassed a similar academic record at Brown University, graduating *summa cum laude* in 1928. For the next four years, he studied medicine at Harvard, and during the depths of the Great Depression, was granted his M.D. degree in 1932. In the succeeding four years, Seebert underwent intensive training in surgery as a resident physician at Beth Israel Hospital, Boston; Boston City Hospital, Charles V. Chapin Hospital, Providence, and Mt. Sinai Hospital, New York City.

In 1936, Seebert returned to Providence, the city of his birth, to establish himself in general surgery. Six years later, after the United States entered World War ll, he set aside his practice to volunteer. Following the customary military indoctrination, Capt. Goldowsky was assigned to the Southwest Pacific Theater of Operations for the remainder of the conflict. His was a distinguished military career. He participated in three major inland campaigns between 1942 to 1945.

By 1946, Seebert was back in Providence as a civilian surgeon. His principal institutional affiliation now included Rhode Island Hospital, where he was director of their peripheral vascular disease clinic, and The Miriam Hospital, where he was chief of surgery.

In 1958, Seebert began a productive association with Blue Cross Blue Shield of R.I., which culminated in his appointment as their medical director.

Seebert was one of the first practicing surgeons in this community to be appointed to the clinical faculty at Brown University's new medical school. He was also chosen to serve as president for numerous professional societies, councils and associations, including the medical staff of The Miriam Hospital and the Council of the New England Medical Society.

His productive career also included the editorship of the state medical journal, a position which he held for 27 uninterrupted years. Managing this monthly publication required that he write numerous editorials concerning medical ethics, recent advances in therapies, newly devised procedures, vignettes on medical history and warnings when he perceived a threat to the integrity of his profession. These editorials, collectively numbering over 1,000, served as a constant reminder to the practicing physicians that the high moral standards of the medical profession required constant vigilance. Seebert, as far back as 1950, was instrumental in alerting Rhode Island physicians to the mortal dangers of cigarette smoking. And in the succeeding decades he led the local crusade against the use of tobacco.

In 1959, Seebert began yet another component of his richly varied and productive life. At that time he published an essay providing an historic account of the Jewish Orphanage of Rhode Island. During the succeeding 35 years he authored numerous papers on local Jewish history and culture. These articles appeared in the *Rhode Island Jewish Historical Notes*, a regular periodical which, for a time, he edited. Seebert's major writings also included a seminal biography of Usher Parsons, M.D. (*Yankee Surgeon: The Life and Times of Usher Parsons, 1788-1868*), as well as the definitive history of Providence's Temple Beth-El and its congregation (*A Century and a Quarter of Spiritual Leadership: The Story of the Congregation of the Sons of Israel and David*). In all of these editorial efforts and writings he was materially aided by Bonnie, his wife and closest friend.

There is a curious myth, probably proposed by non-surgeons, that surgeons are characteristically unscholarly, laconic and inept as writers; this, despite the fact that so many of the foremost physician-writers in this country (Seltzer, Nuland, Cushing) are card-carrying surgeons.

With his passing, this community has lost a fine surgeon, author, counselor, administrator – and by his dignity and scrupulous ethical behavior – a wonderful model for succeeding generations of Rhode Island physicians.

Certainly in Rhode Island's recent history there are few physicians who have contributed so materially to the medical profession.

Photo courtesy Dr. Hamolsky

Dr. Milton Hamolsky

Milton W. Hamolsky, M.D.:
Four decades of leadership

A decade before Brown University's medical school became a reality, Brown already had a professor of medicine.

Back in 1963, Rhode Island Hospital recognized that its future as a tertiary care medical center, as well as its contemplated role in providing a site for the clinical training of medical students, depended upon the recruitment of a full-time director of an internal medicine service.

This appointment would represent the first crucial step in transforming the hospital from a community institution managed by physicians in private practice to one with an expanded role to include medical and health care education at all levels, basic and applied research as well as rigorous supervision of the care rendered to its patients. The appointment of a director of internal medicine is typically the first critical undertaking in the transition of a community hospital to an academic medical center.

A search committee examined the credentials of many physician-candidates for this critical post. They finally selected a 42-year-old Massachusetts physician, then an assistant professor of medicine at the Harvard Medical School and an attending physician at Boston's Beth Israel Hospital. His name was Milton William Hamolsky.

Hamolsky was born in Lynn, Mass. (and not Milton, Mass., as some of his admirers have claimed). He was the son of a local shopkeeper and a member of a closely knit family that cherished learning above all other graces. Milton (named after his grandfather, Mordecai) attended Harvard College graduating *summa cum laude*. He then transferred to Harvard Medical School in 1943.

The nation was in the depths of World War ll and medical education was accordingly shorn of all its summer vacations, thus accelerating the process of educating future physicians to three years. Hamolsky received his medical degree in 1946 and his diploma bore those seldom-imprinted words, *magna cum laude,* signifying his station as the school's outstanding student, first in his class.

In the summer of 1946, Hamolsky entered into a long and productive relationship with Beth Israel Hospital, beginning with an internship on the medical service, followed by a three-year medical residency which culminated in his appointment as chief resident physician in medicine.

In the midst of his graduate training, Hamolsky entered the armed services and was assigned to the Army Medical Research Facility at Fort Knox, Kentucky, where he conducted extensive investigations on the diagnostic and therapeutic uses of newly devised radioactive chemicals in a variety of human diseases. He was discharged in 1950, with the rank of captain, returning then to his beloved Beth Israel Hospital. In 1951, he was appointed both to the hospital's attending staff and, concurrently, to Harvard's Dept. of Medicine. And for the succeeding decade he established himself as one of the hospital's authorities on endocrine diseases, particularly ailments of the thyroid gland. By 1958, he was promoted to chief of endocrinology and assistant professor of medicine at Harvard.

During much of this productive interlude, Hamolsky invested his spare time in studying the role of iodine in the metabolism of the thyroid gland, both in normal and abnormal conditions. This investigation was so promising that the Commonwealth Foundation underwrote a research fellowship allowing Hamolsky to devote an entire year (1961-62) to his investigative pursuits. He chose the College de France, in Paris, to undertake this research, which led to the discovery of a laboratory test, used to this day, as a standard diagnostic procedure in determining the status of thyroid function. This research brought him to the attention of medical centers beyond Boston. And, in1963, Rhode Island Hospital recruited him as their physician-in-chief, a position he held until 1987.

And what had he accomplished on behalf of Rhode Island Hospital during those 24 years?

He maintained a superb residency training program, certainly the finest in Rhode Island and one of the best in New England. There are, here in Rhode Island and elsewhere in the United States, hundreds of practicing internists who learned both their clinical skills and their high ethical standards from Milton Hamolsky. In addition, he recruited outstanding full-time chiefs of the subspecialties of internal medicine, including cardiology, pulmonary, gastroenterology, nephrology and other disciplines. And in doing so, he created the groundwork for a multidisciplinary clinical service that could easily accommodate the educational needs of a medical school. Brown, in its wisdom, appointed him as professor of medicine despite the absence of any medical school in 1963 or even a corporate commitment to create a medical school in the foreseeable future.

Hamolsky's contributions to health care in Rhode Island extended beyond the portals of the Rhode Island Hospital. He was senior consultant to The Miriam Hospital and the Veterans Administration Hospital, served concurrently as chief at Women and Infants Hospital, worked on countless committees under the aegis of the state government, the state medical society and private organizations such as Planned Parenthood of R.I. During those active years he also served as presidents of the R.I. Heart Association and the R.I. Diabetes Association and governor of the American College of Physicians.

The internal medicine service of the Rhode Island Hospital, under Hamolsky's leadership, has now provided the core inpatient experience for 30 consecutive classes of Brown medical students. And, in rotation with his colleagues at the other Brown teaching hospitals, he had taken on the additional responsibilities of chairing Brown University's Department of Medicine.

In 1987, Hamolsky retired but only to assume yet another heavy responsibility as chief administrative officer of the state's Board of Medical Licensure and Discipline. Under his inspired stewardship, the board has been transformed into a superbly managed agency that has become a model for other states to emulate. And when the directorship of the R.I. Dept. of Health became vacant, it was Hamolsky who was called upon to briefly assume its leadership.

This month (Jan. 2002), Dr. Milton Hamolsky will finally retire as a practicing physician. He has given Rhode Island almost four decades of dedicated and exemplary leadership as an administrator, as teacher, and as wise and humane practitioner. Rhode Island, its local medical school and its teaching hospitals, are collectively indebted to that anonymous search committee which, some 40 years ago, brought a gifted physician named Hamolsky to this community.

Tribute to an obscure Israeli physician

If they achieved little else, the depression years of the 20th century left us with enduring memories. Those early depression years witnessed bank failures, families evicted from their homes for failure to pay rent, soup kitchens on major street corners and ill-clad men wandering the streets at midday seeking itinerant employment. But there was also a fragile sense of hope that the recent election of President Franklin D. Roosevelt might counteract the economic and emotional despondency which gripped the nation in 1932.

From Cluj he traveled by foot to Moldavia in the east, found his way into the Ukraine which was overrun by advancing German troops in 1941, and joined the refugee masses all attempting to survive.

In the Brooklyn tenement where I lived as a teenager, we learned the principles and exigencies of food shortages the hard way. And yet I also vividly recall that there were always two small tin boxes on our kitchen table, somewhere near the salt cellar. One can bore the name Palestine in pale blue letters and the other was nameless. Every week we would deposit into each can the few coins that the family could spare. The money in the named receptacle was then forwarded to the Jewish National Fund to support the development of the Land of Israel, and the other was to support my mother's brother in Czernowitz, Romania, particularly his ailing wife and son, my cousin Hugo.

During the 1930s my mother would go to the local post office each month to purchase postal money orders which were then faithfully mailed to the old country. And each month we received word from Europe of Cousin Hugo's educational progress, how well he did and finally, in 1936, when he was admitted to medical school in the city of Cluj, in northern Romania.

When war arrived in Europe on the first day of September 1939, my family lost contact with Hugo and his family. The years that followed were years of silence and increasing anguish that Hugo and his family had become victims of the Romanian fascist government. And when Germany invaded the Soviet Union in the summer of 1941, occupying Romania in the process, we were convinced that Hugo and his family had been consumed by the spreading Holocaust.

In the early spring of 1946, when I was returning from the Army, I received a call from my mother excitedly exclaiming, "Hugo is alive!" The family gathered to review a brief and cryptic letter that my mother had received, postmarked from Turkey, written by Hugo and with little information as to where he had been during the seven terrible years of silence, how he managed to get to Turkey, where he was currently living or whether his parents were yet alive. The family had no way of communicating with him and the weeks that followed were weeks of anguish.

Months passed with no further word from Hugo and during that interval we learned from other sources that Hugo's family back in Czernowitz were all victims of the Holocaust. Hugo's letter, by then a precious family document, was read and reread during the months of silence. Early in 1947 we finally received word from Hugo, now postmarked from the Palestinian Mandate, indicating that Hugo had managed to travel through Syria and French-held Lebanon, to cross into British-controlled Palestine. He reported that he was in reasonably good health but had no possessions except for a very precious document that he had preserved in a waterproof container bound to his chest. It was, of course, his diploma from the university in Cluj, indicating that that he was the possessor of the M.D. degree.

In the years that followed, Hugo joined the Israeli Defense Force serving honorably, then married a refugee from Austria, established a family-oriented practice of medicine in the city of Gedera and enlarged his family with the births of two sons.

Hugo Hassner never aspired to achieve academic recognition in Israel. He practiced his medical art with a sense of humility and commitment, never joining any of the medical faculties or the staffs of any of the impressive hospitals of his nation. Yet within Gedera he was revered as a devoted practitioner of medicine who spoke a badly accented but earnest Hebrew. One of his sons joined the Israeli diplomatic corps and the other became a physician in the field of endocrinology.

Where was he from 1939 to '46? From Cluj he traveled by foot to Moldavia in the east, found his way into the Ukraine which was overrun by advancing German troops in 1941, and joined the refugee masses all attempting to survive. His newly developed medical skills probably kept him alive in the vast refugee gatherings of the southern Ukraine; and when the war ended he found his way to northern Turkey across the Black Sea. By 1947 he survived yet another trek into British Palestine.

My mother, who died in 1963, was never well enough to make the trip to Israel, but she received an abundance of letters from her nephew, Hugo, always beginning with the tender words, "Leibe Tante Lena."

My daughter, Sarah, received her M.D. degree in 1987 and after a year of medical internship in Connecticut, resolved to practice in Israel for two years. One of her first actions, of course, was to visit my cousin Hugo. They spent much time together and shared many family stories, both happy and sad.

I visited Israel for the first time in 1989, eagerly anticipating a visit with Hugo. But coronary disease has neither sentiment nor respect for hallowed memory and Hugo died before we met. I am heartened by the reality that Hugo's life was fulfilled and that he and Sarah, after more than half a century, reunited the family.

Metchnikoff: Unlocking the secrets of starfish

They described him as a large man; broad of shoulders, ample in girth, abundantly bearded, who spoke French with a distinct Russian accent.

His full name was Ilya Ilich Mechnikov (or Metchnikoff) but friends and family called him Elie. He was born in 1845 in the Ukranian village of Ivanovka in the shadow of the ancient city of Kharkov. His education in developmental biology

> *There are those who still subscribe to his belief that a diet principally of yogurt is life-prolonging.*

was completed at the Kharkov State University in 1864 and he was then appointed a professor of zoology at the University of Odessa where he taught, and quietly undertook some basic research, for the next 12 years.

In 1882, he was invited to Messina, Italy, where he worked on the embryology of a family of marine invertebrates including the starfish. It was with these primitive creatures that Metchnikoff made his first and most significant discovery.

In observing the structural development of the starfish, from its embryonic beginnings as a cluster of cells to its maturity, he noted some rounded, mobile, microscopic cells, which didn't seem to fulfill any obvious function. Metchnikoff's inquisitive mind suggested an experiment: he injected a small quantity of a red dye into the interior of a living, adult starfish to see how, or even whether, these unknown cells would react. To his delight, under the microscope they reacted promptly and energetically by eating the fragments of the dye. Using Greek roots he coined a name for his discovery: "phagocytes" (cells which devour). Metchnikoff expanded his studies on the mysterious phagocytes to demonstrate that a wide range of creatures, including man, were endowed with them, that they were located in tissues beyond the blood vessels and that they were also found in the white blood cells.

Metchnikoff entered into an extended debate with research pathologists who believed that these cells were merely passive carriers of foreign material such as germs (germs could sometimes be demonstrated within the interior of phagocytes). Metchnikoff's contention was that the cells were active defenders of the body, absorbing and ultimately destroying alien invaders such as bacteria. Repeated experiments finally validated his thesis that these cells were crucial to the body's integrity.

Pasteur Institute director

In 1887, Metchnikoff was invited to join the prestigious Pasteur Institute in Paris and in 1895, he was chosen as its director. During the two succeeding decades Metchnikoff's research in the elements of the body's vital defenses – in a new field which he called cellular immunology – flourished, and with a German scientist named Paul Ehrlich, he was awarded the Nobel Prize in Medicine and Physiology in 1907. Ehrlich maintained that specific proteins in the globulin fraction of the blood stream – which we now call them antibodies – were crucial in protecting the human body against bacterial and viral invasion. Ehrlich's inaugural research and Metchnikoff's discoveries combined to found the critically important field of clinical immunology, with an indispensable, collaborative role played by both the phagocytes of the body and the proteins called antibodies.

Metchnikoff's phagocytes turned out to be more than cells with an appetite for foreign invaders. He found that these cells could, over time, increase their immune response to a specific bacterium in a host.

Working closely with the great French research bacteriologist, Roux, Metchnikoff's experiments aided researchers to understand the complexities of syphilis and a means by which newer anti-syphilitic drugs might be evaluated. Metchnikoff's work in succeeding years dealt with many fundamental components of human biology and human responses to infectious disease.

Demographic studies

Metchnikoff later developed an interest in why some people lived longer than others. His demographic studies led him to certain villages in Bulgaria where, despite great poverty, many people lived beyond the age of 90. He speculated that the operative factor might be their curious diet. He noted that many lived principally on a soured milk product called yogurt. His research isolated a harmless germ called lactobacillus, which may have provided some form of bodily protection. His early findings indicated that this bacillus might have a suppressive effect on other, harmful germs.

Metchnikoff died in 1916 at age 71, in the midst of World War I, before his progress in the biology of aging (a field that he called gerontology), had advanced very far. There are those who still subscribe to his belief that a diet principally of yogurt is life-prolonging.

In his final years, Metchnikoff wrote some philosophically oriented texts on the nature of man. One of his last reflections concerned the role of science: "If there can be formed an ideal able to unite men in a kind of religion of the future, this ideal must be founded on scientific principles. And if it be true, as has been asserted so often, that man can live by faith alone, the faith must be in the power of science."

Albert Sabin, the savior from Bialystok

Bialystok, a small city in the northeastern corner of Poland, has at least three claims to fame: It is the culinary home of the bialy, the lead character (Max Bialystock) in Mel Brooks' great comedy, "The Producers," and most importantly, it is the birthplace of Albert Sabin.

Sabin was born Aug. 26, 1906, to Tillie and Jacob Sabin. Unsettled conditions in the Baltic region following the 1917 revolution in Russia led to the hasty migration of the Sabin family to Patterson, N.J., where Albert, 11, rapidly learned English. After some college courses, young Sabin matriculated at the New York University School of Medicine and received his medical degree in 1931.

Instead of a clinical career, Sabin pursued his abiding interest in infectious diseases and worked for a decade at the Rockefeller Institute for Medical Research. When the United States entered World War ll, in December of 1941, Sabin joined the U.S. Army and was assigned to the Epidemiological Board, where his creative labors led to the development of a vaccine to combat dengue fever. Sabin, now a lieutenant colonel, was also instrumental in devising a vaccine for Japanese encephalitis.

Following the war, he joined the medical faculty of the University of Cincinnati as a professor of pediatrics, where he researched viral diseases, particularly poliomyelitis. There are two critical steps in the development of a vaccine: isolating the causative agent and then modifying it so that it is no longer infectious (usually by killing it with chemicals), while not disturbing its capacity to elicit an immune reaction in the host. It is then injected into humans in the hope that it will stimulate an immune response without actually causing the disease.

Sabin was impressed with the curious fact that polio was rampant in the more sanitary and developed urban communities of Europe and America and virtually absent in the populations of Africa and Asia. He speculated that conditions in these poorer communities were so unsanitary that virtually all infants were infected with the virus (via the intestinal system) shortly after birth. They did not develop paralysis because the virus never got beyond the gut in infants and because there might be errant strains that did not infect the whole body and were biologically incapable of producing paralysis. But, Sabin then speculated, if these non-paralytic strains could be isolated and then propagated in the laboratory, might they not be used as a live vaccine to produce immunity in potential victims of polio? In essence, Sabin was proposing the radical notion of infecting children with a strain of polio that produced, at worst, a mild and transitory diarrhea.

Sabin's worldwide search for non-paralytic strains of polio succeeded, and although Salk's vaccine was first tried successfully in 1956, Sabin endeavors finally succeeded in 1958 when the oral vaccine was tested in prison volunteers successfully. In 1960, Sabin undertook a massive field trial when some 80 million people, mostly children, in Mexico, Russia and Africa were given the oral vaccine. The trials were hugely successful; immunity was rapidly achieved without secondary complications or the need for injections, since the Sabin vaccine was administered by mouth in a teaspoon of sugared water. Sabin's vaccine also resulted in lifelong immunity while the Salk vaccine required periodic booster injections. The first mass testing in this country was on April 24, 1960, when many millions of children were given the vaccine on what historians call "Sabin Sunday."

Today, the western hemisphere and all of Western Europe are free of clinical poliomyelitis. The World Health Organization hopes to eradicate it totally by 2007. It is estimated that the work of Salk and Sabin has, since the 1950s, saved well over a million lives and prevented untold millions of cases of disabling limb paralysis.

Sabin continued his research endeavors at Cincinnati. He also concurrently accepted the presidency of the Weizmann Institute in Rehovot, Israel, in 1970. He pursued his research interests beyond the age of 80. Numerous universities paid tribute to his immense scientific efforts with honorary degrees. In 1986, the United States conferred on him this nation's highest civilian award, the Presidential Medal of Freedom. Sabin continued to lecture widely, promoting his view that the nations of the world should now join to conquer "diseases of ignorance."

Failing health caused him to retire at age 85 and he died in 1993 at age 87. The "boychik" from Bialystok had accomplished what few aspiring scientists could ever dream of. Sabin and "the kid from the Bronx," Jonas Salk, had saved the lives of millions who probably never heard of either Bialystok or the Bronx.

The man who invented chemotherapy

Germany, in the post-Napoleonic decades of the 19th century, was a collection of contiguous principalities stretching from the North Sea to the western margins of imperial Russia. Toward the northeast was a region called Upper Silesia, with Breslau as its administrative and cultural center. South of Breslau was the town of Strehlen with a small but established Jewish community. Ismar Ehrlich and his wife, Rose Weigert Ehrlich, owned a small clothing manufacturing plant in the town.

He initiated that branch of applied biology now called immunology, and his imaginative genius led inevitably to the life-preserving science called chemotherapy. He was awarded the Nobel Prize in Medicine in 1908.

A son named Paul was born to the Ehrlichs on March 14, 1854. He was given a fine elementary and secondary education in Breslau, attended its university, and then went on to the university in Freiburg-am-Main, where he was granted his medical degree in 1878.

Most European medical schools required that their students write, and then defend, a research thesis, usually on some clinical subject, before the doctorate degree is conferred. Paul Ehrlich chose to investigate a group of newly isolated chemicals derived from coal tar, called the aniline dyes. The British chemist, W. Perkin, had recently demonstrated that certain aniline derivatives functioned as coloring agents, thus creating a major new industry for the dyeing of fabrics. Ehrlich's interest in the aniline dyes, however, was confined to their capacity to attach themselves to certain microscopic structures but not to others within animal cells. In a curiously prescient way, his fascination with these distinctive staining characteristics of aniline chemicals, called affinities, hinted at the direction of his future research work, which led ultimately to the field of chemotherapy.

Following graduation, Ehrlich worked in the Berlin Medical Clinic but devoted much time to research in the bacteriology laboratory of his cousin, the eminent bacteriologist Karl Weigert.

Ehrlich's obsession with dyes led to the discovery that certain dyes brilliantly outlined the microscopic structures of the white blood cells, distinguishing one from another. His biological stains became the standard laboratory method for the clinical examination of human blood. By 1882, Ehrlich's fascination with chemicals that had an affinity for certain chemicals in cells led him to discover a means by which the bacillus that caused tuberculosis could readily be made visible by microscopy.

In 1887, Ehrlich developed pulmonary tuberculosis and moved to the dry climate of Egypt for two years until he had fully recovered. He returned to Berlin, now working with Robert Koch, the scientist who had discovered the causative agent of both tuberculosis and cholera. In the next few years, Ehrlich elaborated on his theories concerning the nature of human immunity and how the body reacts to and neutralizes toxins. His seminal research did much to establish a newly evolving science called immunology.

The German government, recognizing his investigative genius, established a specific research institute for him to study the nature of immunity and to find ways of standardizing vaccines and antisera.

In 1897, Ehrlich accepted a government invitation to move to Frankfurt-am-Main as director of the newly established Royal Institute of Experimental Therapy. The Speyer family, locally involved in the dyeing industry, then established a separate research facility adjacent to the institute (the famous *Speyerhaus*), allowing Ehrlich free rein in his research pursuits.

Ehrlich harked back to his earlier research indicating that chemicals, such as the aniline dyes, did not color objects merely by coating them much like paint upon a flat surface. Rather, the microscopic structures, whether human cells or cotton fibers, had selective chemical receptors which would join solely with these chemicals. He defined the chemical nature of this reaction and saw its analog in the specific action of an antitoxin combining with a toxin.

Using an industrial dye called trypan red, he found that it attached itself, and partially destroyed, the parasite of trypanosomiasis, the causative agent of sleeping sickness. This chemical thus became the first agent capable of alleviating a specific infectious disease.

The last decade of the 19th century witnessed the accelerated growth of bacteriology. Many infectious diseases were now shown to be caused by specific micro-organisms, one of them being the scourge of syphilis. Ehrlich conjectured: "Might it be possible to find a chemical which, when introduced into the body, would attach itself solely to the surface of the microbe in question, fatally injuring that microbe, while not affecting any of the body's tissues?" He called such a hypothetical chemical a "magic bullet" and he then directed his laboratory to investigate an immense variety of chemicals, beginning with the trivalent arsenicals.

The 606th trial (the number 606 has now become enshrined in the annals of medical history) worked effectively against the germs of syphilis and thus was born the drug salvarsan. Ehrlich persevered, since salvarsan proved to be somewhat toxic. And, by trial number 914 in 1907, a better agent was identified: a drug now called neosalvarsan. Ehrlich, never without his cigars (he smoked about 25 lengthy cigars a day) now enunciated his belief that some day each infectious disease would prove to be vulnerable to the combining action of a specific chemical, a process that he now chose to call chemotherapy.

Ehrlich, given the freedom to follow the investigative paths of his choosing, gave the world an entirely new, chemically-based concept of how the human body defends itself against the invasion of alien organisms such as bacteria. He initiated that branch of applied biology now called immunology, and his imaginative genius led inevitably to the life-preserving science called chemotherapy. He was awarded the Nobel Prize in Medicine in 1908. The onset of a world war in 1914 distressed him deeply, principally because of his pacifist beliefs. A stroke incapacitated him in 1915 and shortly thereafter another stroke caused his death. The research institute in Frankfurt still exists; its street name has been changed to *Ehrlichstrasse*.

Jonas Salk, medical sleuth and scientist

When their first son was born on Oct. 28, 1914, the Salks named him Jonas, a curious and rarely used spelling for the name of the minor prophet Jonah. Jonas, which in Hebrew means the dove, indeed was a quiet and reflective child.

The family, who lived in the Bronx, was poor. Jonas' parents, both immigrants from czarist Russia, worked in the garment industry in New York City, and the choice of Jonas' college was therefore narrowed to City College of New York, a tuition-

> *The influenza virus had recently been isolated, and working with Dr. Thomas Francis, Salk undertook the immense task of devising an influenza vaccine for the United States Army.*

free municipal institution in upper Manhattan. His original intention had been to prepare himself for a career in the law but exposure to the mysteries of biology led him to think, rather, of medicine.

Salk's grades at City College were outstanding but the family could not meet the additional expenses, including board and lodging, of an out-of-city medical school. Accordingly, Salk applied for and was accepted to the School of Medicine at New York University in Manhattan. He lived at home and met his modest tuition costs through scholarship and after-class employment.

Of the many aspects of human disease that Salk encountered as a medical student, the physiological intricacies of the immune response to pathogens fascinated him the most. His absorption in immunology was so intense that he was granted a year off solely to pursue research work in the chemistry of vaccines.

Upon graduation from medical school, Salk completed the customary internship training at Mount Sinai Hospital in New York City. But then he left the arena of clinical medicine to join the University of Michigan Medical School basic sciences faculty, to conduct research on influenza vaccines. The influenza virus had recently been isolated, and working with Dr. Thomas Francis, Salk undertook the immense task of devising an influenza vaccine for the United States Army. Their efforts were successful and by 1947 Salk accepted a research professorship at the University of Pittsburgh, heading their virus research laboratory to further study vaccine programs.

The Foundation for Infantile Paralysis, more commonly known as the March of Dimes, through its director Basil O'Connor, expressed interest in Salk's theory that a vaccine composed of killed virus particles might be as effective as a vaccine of modified, virulent virus particles. It had been believed that any laboratory manipulation of viruses would so alter its capacity to elicit an immune response as to make it ineffective as a vaccine. Salk believed otherwise, and by minimally altering the poliomyelitis virus through exposure to formaldehyde, he believed that the resulting vaccine, devised from the killed virus, would prove to be both immunologically effective and clinically safe.

The Foundation then chose to underwrite Salk's research protocol and for the next five years he labored to perfect a safe vaccine. Both he and the Foundation were under immense public pressure to hasten the development of this vaccine. In 1952, for example, 57,628 Americans, mainly children, were newly afflicted with paralytic poliomyelitis, making it the worst year on record for this dread disease. That same year, using a trial form of the vaccine, Salk inoculated a small group of volunteers, including his three sons, his wife and himself. The results were encouraging and a massive inoculation campaign was then undertaken in 1953 with 1.83 million children receiving the Salk vaccine. In the following year his results were published in the *Journal of the American Medical Association*, and on April 12, 1955, a number of monitoring committees jointly declared the injectable vaccine to be both safe and effective.

Salk then endeared himself to a vast public when he refused to patent the vaccine and thus did not profit from his discoveries.

The modest origins of penicillin

Louis Pasteur once commented, "In the fields of observation, chance favors the mind that is prepared." The gifted scientist, Pasteur contended, is not luckier than his more pedestrian colleagues; rather, he is more sensitive to the potential ramifications of some oddity seen but ignored by most others. The history of science is full of insightful researchers who have translated chance observations into monumental discoveries.

Consider a Scottish physician named Alexander Fleming, working in St. Mary's Hospital, London, as its microbiologist. He left for a weekend one Friday, inadvertently leaving on his laboratory bench an open petri dish with cultures of staphylococci germs. When he returned on Monday, the dish was additionally contaminated with an ordinary airborne mold, which had grown luxuriantly. But, he noted, the staphylococci colonies near the mold had all disappeared, while those at a distance from the mold continued to proliferate. Fleming surmised that the mold was generating a substance which inhibited or actually killed the staphylococcal germs. He pursued this research, and in 1929, published a paper on the anti-bacterial qualities of this mold (or fungus) named *Penicillium notatum*. Fleming's penicillium mold produced so little of the anti-bacterial substance that he did not choose to investigate it further, considering it a scientific curiosity of marginal interest. He nevertheless published his curious observation in a widely read medical journal.

The onset of World War II provoked the scientific establishment in England to seek better ways of containing battlefield infections. Those in charge of the military were painfully aware that contaminated wounds killed many more soldiers than did enemy bullets. Therefore, a major effort was initiated to recruit scientists to seek out ways of containing, or even curing, bacterial infections which arose in the course of warfare.

Dr. Howard Florey, a scientist at Oxford University, was asked to assemble a team to investigate a number of promising leads. He immediately recruited several outstanding scientists from the Oxford faculty, including Drs. Ernst Boris Chain, Norman Heatley, E.P. Abraham and Mary Florey.

Chain had been working on an antibacterial substance in human tear drops, something called lysozyme, which had also been discovered by Fleming. Remembering Fleming's 1929 publication, Chain and Florey proposed that they investigate the substance elaborated by penicillium which, until then, had proved to be unstable and could only be produced in minute quantities.

Some strains of penicillium produced no antibacterial substance; others so little as to be worthless in producing a meaningful medication. A worldwide search for more productive strains of penicillium was hastily undertaken, and a research technician in Peoria, Ill., (later called "Moldy Mary") scoured her local grocery stores, finding innumerable moldy fruits and vegetables to be sent back to the Chain and Florey laboratories. She chanced upon a moldy cantaloupe, which eventually generated more of the anti-bacterial substance than other strains of penicillium.

Chain, back at Oxford, devised ways of increasing its yield, stabilizing it and ultimately determining its chemical structure. Florey then undertook field experiments with the substance distilled by Chain, now called penicillin. A London policeman with a massive infection was the first recorded subject of their experiment. The patient seemed to recover but relapsed and died. It was surmised that insufficient penicillin had been given. But now, with laboratories in both England and the United States growing a higher-yield penicillium, increasing amounts of penicillin were made available. And, both in experimentally infected mice and in humans with natural infections, penicillin proved to be a miraculous agent, the first of a new family of medications called antibiotics.

Fleming, Chain and Florey were awarded the Nobel Prize in Medicine in 1945.

Chain was born in 1906 in Berlin to Russian refugee parents. He was educated at Friedrich-Wilhelm University, majoring in chemistry. He was then employed at the Charite Hospital in Berlin, where he devised numerous laboratory procedures for the isolation and identification of enzymes.

With the arrival of the Nazi regime in Germany, Chain fled to England, finding work in the biochemistry department at Cambridge University. His family had chosen not to emigrate and they all died in the Holocaust.

Chain's innovative discoveries concerning the chemistry of snake venoms and the metabolism of tumor cells caught the attention of the senior faculty at Oxford University. In 1935 he was invited to join the Sir William Dunn School of Pathology. It was there that he met Florey and they embarked on a quest for a feasible antibiotic; culminating in two major accomplishments: First, the development of technical methods to achieve substantial amounts of penicillin, (and eventually by discovering the chemical structure of penicillin, to synthesize the substance in factories) and secondly, to demonstrate in rigorously supervised clinical field tests, that penicillin in adequate dosage can cure previously mortal infections caused by a variety of micro-organisms.

Chicken soup is sometimes humorously called "Jewish penicillin." Ironically, the seminal contributions in the discovery of penicillin were by a refugee Jewish chemist named Boris Chain.

Chapter 7
The witch of Endor

Foretelling the future by means of omens, soothsaying, incantations, altar sacrifices or divination has always been an uncertain enterprise. The nomadic Hebrews regarded such conjuring acts as abominations and expressly forbade them (Lev. 19:28). Appealing to ghosts or making inquiries of familiars (Lev. 19: 31) was also construed as an act of personal defilement. (A familiar, from the Latin, *familius*, was defined as a servant and specifically a servant, such as a witch, beholden to the devil.)

For the Israelites, the long exodus after the Egyptian exile represented a transformation of their nomadic society from a people seduced by pagan ritual to a monotheistic culture committed to a set of moral laws. And while the Books of Moses celebrate the faithful adherence of many to the Mosaic code, they also relate the numberless episodes of regression to idolatry and necromancy.

Witches (or their male counterparts, called wizards) do not appear prominently in the Scriptures. But during the troubled reign of King Saul (I Samuel 28:7) a sad and intensely human tragedy unfolds. Saul is fearful of the impending battle with the numerically superior Philistines, who are arrayed in great masses before the slopes of Gilboa. The prophet Samuel has died and Saul no longer can rely upon his perceptive counsel; nor does God respond to Saul's direct appeals. In desperation Saul asks a subordinate to seek out a sorceress to prophesy the outcome of the forthcoming battle. They find such a witch in the Canaanite village of Endor. Saul, disguised, then accosts the witch. At first she resists his demands that she summon the ghost of Samuel from the grave, citing the Israelite injunctions against such heathen acts.

Saul, however, promises her immunity and she finally evokes the spirit of Samuel, who tells Saul that he, as well as his sons, will perish in the ensuing battle. And the prediction comes true.

The occult role of the witch in this tale is confined to bringing forth one who can foretell the future. She entices no virtuous person to paths of evil; she creates no mischief, and the Bible makes no further mention of her.

The Talmud, on the other hand, claims that this witch was Abner's mother and wife to Zephaniah. And, say the Talmudic sages, Saul died with his sons "so that his portion might be with Samuel in the future life and that he might dwell in the prophet's division in heaven."

There is an Islamic version of this story. Saul, in an uncontrollable rage, kills his many wise advisers, but one escapes, the woman of Endor. In remorse, Saul seeks to atone for his sins and goes to this wise woman for counsel. She leads him to the tomb of Samuel and conjures up the prophet's ghost who intones: "Let the King and his sons go down to the city of giants and there they shall fall." And so it was.

Acts of divination abound in Genesis but the notion of a central domain of wickedness manipulating the practitioners of sorcery and other occult acts is not described. Indeed, the concept of a witchcraft conspiracy, with women as the active agents of satanic evil, does not assume prominence until the Middle Ages.

In the late decades of the 15th century, numerous acts of heresy were said to be rampant in the German cities, prompting Pope Innocent VIII to issue a bull detailing the magnitude of this apostasy and sanctioning his representatives to make formal inquiry into such heretical acts. Two prominent clerics, Johann Sprenger and Heinrich Kramer, were appointed to create the legal framework for this inquisition, and in May of 1487 they issued an enabling text called *Malleus Maleficarum* (The Witch's Hammer).

The text was composed of three divisions: The first provided theologic arguments proving the existence of witches and witchcraft; the second offered numerous case reports of acts of *maleficium* – instances of witches doing harm to others by supernatural powers bestowed upon them by the devil – and the third, technical means for the legal identification of witches, technics of torture and means of execution. Killing was justified by a line in Exodus: "Thou shalt not suffer a witch to live."

Most who have read this handbook of the Inquisition agree that it is an uncompromising, sadistic, pitiless and mysogynous polemic. And among its victims, as indicated by the numerous case histories offered, were hapless victims of epilepsy, mental derangement, organic dementia and all manner of neuropsychiatric debility. The tragedy of the Inquisition goes well beyond the destruction of nonconformist faith groups. In their zeal to condemn the heretic, the inquisitors imprisoned, tortured and often executed many neurologically afflicted individuals under the presumption that their souls had been possessed.

The witches of the Biblical era were powerful sorceresses capable of communicating with the dead. But with the exception of the Witch of Endor, few exerted any notable influence upon the affairs of state. Witchcraft assumed prominence only during the last millennium when a satanic domain, with countless human helpers, was evoked to explain the magnitude of evil on this earth. The Inquisition blurred any distinctions between nonconformity and apostasy or between eccentric behavior and heresy. It was an unhappy time when the inexplicable rapidly deteriorated to the sinister. And to explain what had been regarded as a global conspiracy by the forces of the underworld, the concept of the witch, the evil woman, was invoked.

The fear of women is patently evident in the text of Sprenger and Kramer. On page 43 of *Malleus* is written, "What else is woman but a foe to friendship, an unescapable punishment, a necessary evil, a natural temptation, a desirable calamity, a domestic danger, a delectable detriment, an evil of nature, painted with fair colors."

Nor has witch-hunting confined itself to the 15th century. The terrible witchhunts of 17th-century England (and New England) bear witness to the continuing fear, misogyny and innate barbarism which prevailed at that time and perhaps lingers to the present.

In sorrowful labor

In the beginning, "The Lord God said, 'It is not good for man to be alone; I will make a fitting helper for him.'" (Genesis 2:18). "So the Lord God cast a deep sleep upon the man; and while he slept, He took one of his ribs and closed up the flesh at that spot." (Genesis 2:21).

Both loneliness and pain are grievous things; and it was therefore a consummate act of divine mercy to cast a deep and senseless sleep upon this man while a part of his body was removed so that he might then be blessed with the companionship of a woman; an intimate companionship since they were both of one flesh.

The compassionate specialty of anesthesiology, a science that has made deliberate surgery possible, looks to this Scriptural reference as its origin and justification.

What physiological characteristics did medicine demand of a general anesthetic? First, that it rapidly renders the patient unconscious; but an unconsciousness deeper than normal sleep since it must also be accompanied by a total insensitivity to pain. Second, that the process be quickly and readily reversible. And third, that it cause no harm to the brain or other vital organs. It must therefore be a procedure which is rapidly induced, safe and without long-lasting complications.

Conquest of pain and the induction of insensible sleep had been the conscious goal of medicine for millennia. And over the centuries an impressive array of herbal preparations has been tested to induce stupor and insensitivity to pain. Opium products, mandragora root, cannabis and even hemlock were empirically employed to lessen pain and encourage sleep. Prisoners about to be executed by crucifixion were said to be given a concoction of hyssop, mandragora and myrrh in wine or vinegar. Alcohol, too, was widely used to diminish the agonies of orthopedic procedures such as the reduction of bone fractures or joint dislocations.

These many medications were given orally, which meant that their desired effects took time to achieve and sometimes, unexpectedly, produced states of agitation rather than stupefaction. In 1659, Christopher Wren, architect and amateur physiologist, obviated the problem of unreliable absorption of orally given drugs by injecting a combination of opium and wine into a dog's veins, producing a deep stupor. But there were too many hazards encountered with intravenous administration and so this line of research was abandoned.

Induced unconsciousness, for purposes of undertaking some surgical intervention, could also be achieved by temporary compression of the carotid artery in the neck. Intentional blood loss also resulted in collapse and unconsciousness. But these reckless techniques carried such great risk of damage to the body, if not death, that they were also abandoned as ways of producing anesthesia.

It was not until the characteristics and physiological responses to volatile gases were explored that true anesthetic states could be established. Humphrey Davy's primitive experiments with nitrous oxide, in 1800, showed that certain gases might rapidly produce a reversible unconsciousness. Within decades nitrous oxide proved to be of great value in reducing the pain and terror of brief surgical interventions such as dental extractions.

Ether had also been known as a gas capable of producing transient senselessness. Indeed, sniffing vials of ether was a common form of entertainment at medical student parties. And following the success of nitrous oxide, some had suggested that ether, too, might allow more planned surgery measured in minutes rather than seconds. On March 30, 1842, a young Georgia surgeon named Crawford W. Long resected a neck tumor from a patient who had been rendered unconscious by ether. The operation was successful but Long failed to grasp the historic significance of his act and did not report it immediately to his profession. Only four years later, when ether had been employed at Massachusetts General Hospital, did Long belatedly describe his anesthetic experiences.

Ether was administered quite simply by a controlled drip of the fluid upon a cloth pad applied to the patient's nose. Ether vapors were then inhaled, rapidly absorbed through the lungs, thus resulting in a quick suppression of consciousness. Open-drop ether anesthesia was then widely adopted; and the character, status and capabilities of surgery were changed forever.

The success of ether encouraged a search for other volatile fluids which might safely induce unconsciousness. David Waldie, a Liverpool chemist, suggested chloroform to Dr. James Young Simpson, Scotland's leading obstetrician. It was at a dinner party, history tells us, when Simpson fell senseless to the floor after sniffing a small bottle of chloroform. He then successfully eased the pains of child birth by having women in labor inhale the fumes of chloroform. Simpson announced his findings to the world only to be confronted with a virulent outburst of condemnation, largely from the clergy of Great Britain.

These ministers argued that painful childbirth was biblically ordained and that measures undertaken to lessen this anguish were contrary to divine commandment. The unambiguous line, "I will make most severe your pangs in childbearing; in sorrow shall you bear children" (Genesis 3:16), was widely quoted. Simpson was denounced in a blizzard of sermons declaring that his attempts to contravene this scriptural injunction were nothing less than heresy.

But these clergy, scholarly though they were, had not reckoned with the learned Simpson, who was well-schooled in both obstetrics and Biblical Hebrew. Simpson responded promptly, pointing out that the Hebrew word often translated as sorrow also meant labor; that the act of delivery required much labor, and further, that chloroform did not lessen this labor, it merely subdued the subjective appreciation of it.

He further observed, "Those that urge, on a kind of religious ground, that an artificial or anesthetic state of unconsciousness should not be induced...forget that we have the greatest of all examples set before us (Genesis 2:21): 'And the Lord God caused a deep sleep to fall upon Adam; and he slept.' ...This passage is principally striking as affording evidence of our Creator himself using means to save poor human nature from the unnecessary endurance of physical pain."

The outcry against Simpson was promptly stilled in 1853 when he used chloroform to ease the birth of Queen Victoria's son.

The dubious legacy of wine

Long before history was recorded, some nameless ancestor allowed the grape juice from his vineyard to languish; and thus, exposed to the air, it naturally fermented. This prehistoric human then made a remarkable discovery: The banal fruit juice became magically transformed into a sprightly drink capable of loosening the tongue, elevating the spirits and abolishing the insistent cares of the day.

Wine, along with fire and bread, came to be regarded as one of the fundamental gifts bestowed by the gods. Its preparation and storage became a priestly function, and wine was readily incorporated into religious ceremonies.

Wine is cited in the Scriptures over 200 times. Sometimes it is described as a divine gift to mankind, sometimes as a necessary element in some ceremony, sometimes as a means by which well-deserved relaxation might be achieved, and sometimes as a vehicle to lessen grief and alienation.

"Wine maketh glad the heart of man," says the psalmist. And Amos, a sheep breeder during the reign of King Uzziah of Judah, declares, "I will restore my people Israel… They shall plant vineyards and drink their wine." But most Biblical references cast wine rather as an evil, addictive burden upon mankind. In the words of Hosea, "whoredom and wine taketh away the heart."

Given the joyous, sacramental role of wine in so many faiths, current and past, it is intriguing to note the many Biblical tragedies which are ascribed to wine. Indeed, the first mention of wine in Genesis says that Noah, "tiller of soil, was the first to plant a vineyard. He drank of the wine and became drunk, and uncovered himself within his tent." Thus, the inaugural Biblical citation of fermented grape juice, the fruit of the vines, speaks neither of joy nor of conviviality nor even participation in some sacred ritual; rather, it talks of drunkenness and resultant shame.

Further in Genesis is the story of a god-fearing widower named Lot who escaped from Sodom seeking refuge in a remote cave. Then, besodden by wine, Lot slept with his two daughters from which encounter they became pregnant. Thus, the second reference to wine describes it as a drug facilitating incest.

During the stressful, nomadic years in the Sinai desert, the Israelites had little access to wine. Moses spoke the words of the Lord, saying, "I led you through the wilderness 40 years… you had no bread to eat, no wine or other intoxicant to drink…that you might know that I the Lord am your God." This text suggests that only with the clarity of a head free of wine can there be true communion with the divine Spirit.

Also in the Sinai wilderness, the Lord speaks to Aaron, saying, "Drink no wine or other intoxicants, you or your sons, when you enter the tabernacle, that you may not die." This passage has been interpreted to mean that Israelite priests were forbidden to consume wine during holy services.

It is sometimes said that drinking of much wine frees the mind to experience awesome, prophetic visions. Yet when Daniel observes three weeks of mourning, during which time he drinks no wine, he then, and only then, sees "great visions seen by no one else." Later he realizes that the achievement of deeper wisdom can only be attained after a lengthy abstinence.

Each of the prophets has condemned the drinking of intoxicants. Ezekiel talks of the abhorrent deeds undertaken by the people of Israel, practicing deeds of depravity while influenced by wine. On another occasion, Ezekiel berates the Israelites for their blasphemic, wanton harlotries. "You shall be filled with drunkenness and woe," he says, when referring to wine and its "cup of desolation and horror." Isaiah condemns those who begin their drinking binges in the morning, then continue through the night "till wine inflame them." Habbakuk rebukes those who compel still others to drink. Jeremiah censures the Israelites on the use of wine, particularly on the evils of selling wine on the Sabbath. And Obadiah berates those who, "drink till their speech grows thick, and they become as though they had never been."

The Book of Proverbs, that remarkable Scriptural collection of brief reflections, adages and wise insights, contains numerous references to wine, almost all of them unfavorable. "Wine is not for kings…lest they drink and forget what has been ordained and infringe on the rights of the poor." When talking of red wine, Proverbs declares: "In the end it bites like a snake, it spits like a basilisk…your eyes will see strange sights; your heart will speak distorted things." Proverbs suggests, "Do not be of those who guzzle wine or glut themselves on meat; for guzzlers and gluttons will be impoverished, and drowsing will clothe you in tatters." Wine, says the Proverbs, is the drink of futility, for those who are hapless, impoverished, lost and embittered.

There is a wealth of secular poetry alluding to wine as an uplifting, inspiring, gleeful and relaxing fluid, encouraging friendship, diminishing pain and banishing the harsh woes of the world. But wine and other alcoholic intoxicants have their shadowed sides: the destructive world of chronic alcoholism, the carnage of auto accidents, the homes broken by excessive drinking, the many lives shortened.

There is a curious myth that alcoholism is not found amongst Jews. But the many Biblical warnings against drinking suggest that excessive consumption of wine was a problem even in ancient days. And while chronic alcoholism is indeed more frequent in non-Jews, it is a grave error to ignore its existence in Jews. A person's character, says the Talmud, is recognized by three things: how well he tempers his anger, how generous he is, and how much he drinks.

The Bible is history, genealogies, moral allegories, divine poetry, prophetic vision, philosophic reflection and wise instruction. It also seems to be the earliest known text defining the hazards of alcoholism.

The lingering taste of vinegar

A famine spreads over ancient Judea. Elimelekh, his wife, Naomi, and their two sons, Mehlon and Chilion, migrate east to the land of the Moabites to seek food. Elimelekh then dies. The two sons marry local Moabite women, Orpah and Ruth. In time, both sons die leaving Naomi and her two daughters-in-law to fend for themselves. Facing an uncompromising future, Naomi elects to return to Bethlehem and advises Orpah and Ruth to seek new husbands in Moab. But Ruth adamantly remains with Naomi, declaring: "For wherever you go, I will go; your people shall be my people and your God my God." The two women finally arrive in Bethlehem at the onset of the barley harvest, without resources, feeling forsaken and discouraged.

Recognizing the need for food, Ruth decides to glean behind the harvesters of grain. The owner of a field, a man named Boaz and a distant kinsman of Elimelekh, inquires about her and is told of her travails. Boaz declares, "May the Lord reward your deeds." He offers her much barley and asks her to sit at his table, saying: "Come over here and partake of the meal, and dip your morsel in the vinegar."

The story of Naomi and Ruth, the biblical book of Ruth, is a tale of enduring loyalty, integrity and abiding love. Despite famine, perilous migration and the loss of all the males in her adopted family, Ruth survives, and through her eventual marriage to Boaz, begets a son, Obed, who in turn will father Jesse, the father of David, king of Israel. Except for the solitary mention of vinegar, the story provides little detail of the meal offered by Boaz. Indeed, vinegar (*hometz*) is mentioned only four times in the Hebrew Bible (Num. 6:3, Ps. 69:22, Prov. 25-20, Ruth 2:14).

Vinegar represents the final product of a complex process that requires an understanding of the chemical transformations underlying wine production. The existence of a culinary vinegar therefore speaks of a stable culture able to sustain wineries as well as an enterprise which can take wine and deliberately alter it into vinegar.

To the established, non-nomadic cultures of the Middle East, vinegar was substantially more than a flavor-enhancing condiment for meals. It was also an important pharmacological agent employed in the healing of many diseases, a substance used for marinating foods, a cleansing chemical and an additive to water to abate thirst. It was carried routinely by Roman soldiers when on the march and was sometimes given to crucifixion victims as a way to slacken their thirst, as was the case in the New Testament with Jesus (John 19:29).

Sometime in the distant past, a vintner engaged in the conversion of fresh grape juice to wine saw some of his product turn into a sour fluid free of the customary sweet taste of wine, and free, too, of wine's intoxicating qualities. At first, the production of vinegar must have caused dismay to the vintner, but it also yielded a curious fluid with many exploitable properties. It was an acid solution and hence had value as a cleaning agent. But this also posed some hazards. For example, vinegar caused erosion of the surface of teeth (see Proverbs 10:26). Vinegar nevertheless became a dining staple in the cuisine of well-established homes. It provided a pungent, piquant taste to a variety of salad greens and cooked foods.

But it was as a medication that vinegar achieved enduring historic importance. The Talmud carried scores of instructions defining the diverse medical applications of vinegar. For hectic fevers, one was advised to take lentil cakes mixed with vinegar. For intestinal upset, type unspecified, bread soaked in vinegar was suggested. Sipping vinegar periodically was recommended as a way of getting rid of intestinal worms, said the Talmud. Topically applied vinegar was used on all open wounds (presumably as an antiseptic long before sepsis was understood). Migraine headaches, arthritic pains of the hips and even bee stings were said to abate following surface application of vinegar as an antidote to poisonings of botanical origins.

Numerous skin diseases, according to the Talmud, were to be treated with vinegar, either directly upon the skin or in the form of embrocations. The affliction of Job (Job 7:5), sometimes called *shehin*, was said to respond to vinegar applications. And even the malodors of excessive perspiration were thought to diminish following a rinsing with vinegar. Asserting the importance of vinegar, the Talmud declares that a home with neither salt nor vinegar is truly impoverished.

Vinegar was prized during the Middle Ages as a culinary luxury. Its supply was limited to those barrels of wine which turned sour by fortuitous fermentation. Why some wines maintained their quality while other deteriorated to vinegar was not understood. But by the 17th century some French vintners appreciated the commercial value of encouraging wines to ferment to vinegar. They recognized that the thick scum which formed on the surface of sour wine, when intentionally transplanted to other vats of wine, hastened vinegar production. This scum was called *mere de vinaigre* (and the word, vinegar, was derived from the French, *vin aigre*, meaning sour wine). The French also discovered that different flavors and nuances might be developed in vinegars depending on whether the original source was a wine, a beer or a cider. Additional flavors were achieved by fermentation over a bed of balsamic or beechwood shavings.

The mystery of wine and vinegar production was finally clarified in 1864 when Louis Pasteur demonstrated that the conversion of grape juice to an alcoholic beverage was facilitated by the catabolic action of living yeast cells; and further, that certain microorganisms, through oxidation, then converted the alcohol to acetic acid (vinegar).

Vinegar continues today as a widely employed home remedy for a multitude of ills, as a cleaning agent and as a cherished table condiment in many Mediterranean cuisines. In the Book of Ruth, vinegar symbolized the wealth, sophistication and hospitality of Boaz's household.

There is a legend that Cleopatra, to display her boundless wealth, deliberately dissolved a rare pearl in a goblet of vinegar and presented the enriched fluid to her lover to drink. Boaz's more modest sharing of his vinegar with Ruth seems less ostentatious but more compelling and endearing.

The awesome power and authority of blood

In his inaugural statement to the British Parliament on May 13, 1940, Winston Churchill declared: "I have nothing to offer but blood, toil, tears and sweat." He might have cautioned his compatriots to anticipate all manner of bodily harm when he asked them to defend their island, but he settled for blood loss. No culture or religion views blood casually, and certainly bleeding epitomized Churchill's sense of the imminent hazard confronting his imperiled nation. Blood, as metaphor, remains that element of the human body most closely identified with the essence of life. Churchill may also have been thinking of the Scriptures when he uttered those immortal words.

In Genesis, "Cain set upon his brother and killed him." And the Lord declared: "Your brother's blood cries out to me from the ground." To the Hebrews the essence of the soul and the spirit of life rested solely in the blood. Blood was warm, pulsating, and when it was shed, life inevitably fled. More than any tissue, Abel's shed blood was a readily understandable symbol of his departed spirit.

Again in Genesis, the Lord blessed Noah and his sons saying to them that all living creatures were given unto them to eat, but "you must not eat flesh with its life-blood within it." Leviticus provides careful instructions for the slaughter of animals as food, with the stern injunction that the blood of these animals must first be drained, then poured upon the ground and finally covered with earth. Certain Eskimo clans also believe that the blood of slain caribou must be covered with earth for two reasons: first, by returning the blood to Mother Earth, the totality of life is therefore not diminished; and second, that the slayer does not become vulnerable to blood revenge. Blood was clearly the gift of life, a solemn token of God's generosity and not to be consumed or disposed of carelessly.

The covenant between the Lord and Noah, particularly as it pertained to the shedding of human blood and the need for a reckoning, was emphasized in the lines: "Whoever sheds the blood of man, By man shall his blood be shed." (Genesis 9:6.1). Leviticus repeats the commandment: "For the life of the flesh is in the blood."

Blood played a central role in the consecration of the priests of the Hebrews. A ram was sacrificed and some of its blood was then touched to Aaron's right ear, right thumb and right big toe; and the same ritual was then applied to the sons of Aaron in their capacity as priests of the Tent of Meeting. The remainder of the ram's blood was then dashed upon the altar and some intentionally sprinkled on Aaron's cloak. "Thus shall he and his vestments be holy." Leviticus defines the cleansing ritual for someone afflicted with leprosy. The priest, with his right hand, applies blood from a sacrificed animal to the victim's right earlobe, right thumb and right big toe. (The right side of the body, in all cultures dominated by right-handed people, was uniformly regarded as the holier side.)

No society is without its dual taboos and fascinations with blood, even menstrual blood. Primitive hunters drank the blood of both vanquished foes and slain animals of the jungle. Blood of dying gladiators was fought over by spectators in the fervent belief that it would yield renewed strength and potency. Only the ancient Hebrews created commandments forbidding the employment of blood for any communal purpose other than for designated observances.

Certain religious sects take Leviticus at its word. Accordingly, blood transfusions for their adherents, or even use of commercial blood meal to fertilize their flower gardens are forbidden. Over a century ago when blood transfusions had first been routinely employed as life-saving procedures, some clergy wondered whether it was not a covert form of cannibalism.

Blood was also protective. Moses instructed the beleaguered Israelites to sacrifice a lamb and apply its blood to the lintels and doorposts of their homes, "For when the Lord goes through to smite the Egyptians, He will see the blood…and the Lord will pass over the door." (Exodus 12:23). Muslims observed a similar ritual when they smeared the blood of a sacrificed camel upon the lintels of their homes to protect against evil spirits.

Blood has been endowed with many attributes. It has been called impetuous, noble, hot, cowardly, pure, even tainted. Cries for revenge ask typically for blood. (A vengeful demand for lungs or kidneys just lacks suitable passion.) Blood seals covenants, binds close friends as blood-brothers and authenticates contracts. And some disputes require a trial by blood. Blood is central to many sacred rites of redemption, transmutation as well as male initiation ceremonies. Blood even has accusative powers. The Jewish writer, Manasseh ben Israel (1604-1657), wrote that the body of a murdered man will bleed freshly if it is approached by the murderer. And Lady Macbeth's latent sense of guilt was dramatically activated by a small, incriminating spot of blood.

Blood is an integral part of innumerable exclamations, curses, oaths and imprecations.

Blood, according to an old Jewish myth, can recognize kinship. It is said that Solomon, when but a child of 10, adjudicated a claim by demonstrating that the blood of a deceased father could visibly distinguish between a usurper of the family wealth and the rightful son and heir.

"There is no Jewish blood in my veins," declared the contemporary Russian poet, Yevgeny Yevtushenko. It was not at all clear whether he had proclaimed this as a personal lamentation or a declaration of pride, but his statement nonetheless reflects the widespread and ancient belief that blood – more than any other body tissue – carries the substance of personal identity, the essence of heritage and the vital spirit of life. Alternatively, had he exclaimed that his kidneys were not Jewish, he would merely have sounded silly.

There is an old U.S. Army adage offered to those responsible for the training of new recruits: "Tell them what you want them to learn; tell them again; and then tell them what you told them." Tell them, in other words, three times. And three times does Leviticus declare: "Do not partake of blood; for the life of the flesh is in the blood."

The Oath of Asaph and the Hebrew physician

Mention Mount Sinai and most Jews will immediately envision a sophisticated medical center rather than a sacred mountain. This is a natural response since medicine and Judaism, despite discriminatory quotas, have been intimately linked for millennia. Given this historic intimacy, it is therefore surprising to note that physicians are rarely mentioned in the Jewish Bible. Sicknesses, both organic and moral, are, of course, liberally strewn through the Torah, but virtually never the names of the physicians who had treated them. The Bible provides the names of priests, warriors, tenders of sheep, masons, even carpenters of acacia wood but not physicians.

Medicine, during the Pharaonic era, was already an established vocation but had not as yet coalesced into a single healing profession. Instead, there were many parallel endeavors, each offering certain narrowly defined competences. There were the herbalists who provided specific powder, potions and other pharmacologic agents to counteract pertinent ailments. The apothecary art of prescribing botanical and mineral medications persisted in England as a discreet profession until the end of the 19th century. Then there were certain surgically-oriented specialties including the bone-setters (who repaired fractured limbs); the cataract removers; the tooth-pullers; the surgeons who resected bladder stones, lanced abscesses and amputated limbs; and the obstetrical midwives who supervised deliveries or performed abortions. These healers tended to be itinerant artisans who traveled from village to village seeking out customers who might benefit from their narrowly identified skills. And finally, there were those medical practitioners trained selectively in the occult arts of magic, divination and necromancy. The paucity of references to the practice of curative medicine in the Scriptures may reflect three compelling factors. First, in most developing cultures, the art of physician-patient medicine and the functions of divine office were inseparable; both were practiced by members of a priestly caste. These clerics did not distinguish between a secular ailment and someone suffering from a lapse of faith. So it is likely that some medicine had been practiced by the Israelite priests but not to a degree that would merit scriptural comment.

Second, was the divine antagonism, expressed through Moses, toward the idolatrous, magical forms of medicine practiced in Egypt? There are references in the Torah, expressed as commandments, regarding the profane medical practices pursued in Egypt: "You shall not practice divination or soothsaying." (Leviticus 19:26). "Do not turn to ghosts and do not inquire of familiar spirits." (Leviticus 19:31).

And third, was the unambiguous declaration in Scriptures that the continuing health of the nomadic Israelites depended solely on whether they faithfully abided by their code of moral behavior and whether they adhered strictly to the Scriptural Commandments. "If you will heed the Lord your God, diligently, doing what is upright in His sight, giving ear to His Commandments and keeping all his laws, then I will not bring upon you the diseases that I brought upon the Egyptians, for I the Lord am your physician." (Exodus 15:26.1). And in Exodus 23:25: "1 will remove sickness from your midst." With magisterial assurances such as these, what Israelite would possibly demand a second opinion?

Yet somewhere between the time of their exodus through the Sea of Reeds, their 40 years in the intervening wilderness and their arrival at the frontier of the Promised Land, the Israelites developed a set of sophisticated public health regulations which provided them with far more realistic protection against health threats than all the potions, powders and incantations of medicine as practiced in that era.

Medicine, to this day, recognizes the substantive differences between curative medicine and public health medicine. In curative medicine, the initial move is undertaken by the ailing patient. He experiences something abnormal and only then does he seek out the counsel of the physician. The patient shares information about his perceived illness. The physician listens, examines and initiates certain tests to guide him in determining the basis of the patient's distress. He then prescribes some medication or intervention to alleviate the distress.

In public health medicine, on the other hand, all of society is the patient, and the public health physician is more concerned with those interventions which prevent rather than treat illness. If there are any notable advances in health care within the pages of the Bible, it is in the domain of preventive medicine: the need for cleanliness and sanitation within the encampment, the requirement for quarantining carriers of certain communicable illnesses, the advantages of scrupulous personal hygiene, the benefits of food inspection, and the exclusion of certain foods as potential sources of unspecified illness.

In the post-exodus years the reliance by the Israelites upon the Lord as their sole physician must have been tempered by the realization that man had also been endowed with a brain allowing him to understand the enigmatic ways of the world. And if the Lord expected man to seek warmth and shelter in the winter, then certainly he would expect man to seek ways of providing medical care to those in distress.

And by the 6th century CE some sort of organized form of medical practice had evolved for the Hebrews of the Middle East. A physician named Asaph Harofe and Rabbi Yohanan ben Zavda composed an oath, at that time, to be sworn to by the newly trained disciples of medicine.

This Oath of Asaph was written centuries after the Hippocratic Oath and bears some resemblance to it. Some of the precepts in the Oath of Asaph include the following: Do not divulge a man's secret that he has confided unto you; and do not be bribed to do injury and harm and do not harden your heart against the poor and the needy; rather, have compassion upon them and heal them. Do not speak of good as evil, nor of evil as good.

Do not seek after unjust benefit and do not aid the evil-doer to shed innocent blood. Do not mix poison for any man or woman to kill his fellow man, nor disclose their composition; do not give them to any man nor give any devious advice. Do not cause the shedding of blood by essaying any dangerous experiment in the exercise of medical skill; do not cause a sickness in any man.

Little more is known about Asaph or his oath. Had it provided, for example, some guidance when Maimonides wrote his covenantal oath for the newly trained physicians of the 12th century? And how influential was Asaph in the thinking of those physicians who, in the succeeding millennium, fashioned the core of Jewish medical ethics?

Walking: a traditional method of keeping pace with sanctity

For nomadic tribes such as the ancient Hebrews, the ability to walk was as essential to their survival as securing a reliable source of food or water. Those unable to walk, the lame of the community, became a burden, perhaps even a hazard, to a wandering people who depended upon unhindered mobility for their precarious existence.

It should not come as a surprise, then, that the strength to walk unaided was incorporated into many early Hebraic beliefs, religious standards, poetic metaphors, and certainly, criteria for acceptable health.

The Book of Leviticus, probably assembled during the Sinai migration, is uncompromising on the subject of walking. A lame person, regardless of his other qualifications, was not eligible for the priesthood. It made little difference whether his lameness had been secondary to injury, disease or even birth defect.

Who was to be excluded from the priesthood? "No one at all who has a defect shall be qualified: no man who is blind or lame, or has a limb too short or too long." (Leviticus 21:18). Scriptural scholars contend that most ancient societies frowned upon anyone with visible deformity even entering the sacred precincts of their sanctuaries. Yet, it was promised by the prophet Isaiah that the day will arrive when even the lame will have full access to all of the material benefits of earthy existence – but only after the coming of the Redeemer.

In a sect which leaned heavily upon the sanctity of sacrificial rites, even the animals chosen for burnt offerings on the temple altar were required to be free of any blemish or any evidence that they were lame (Leviticus 22:22).

In legend, lameness has sometimes been the price for a direct encounter with God. Jacob, in his struggle with the angel of the Lord, survived, was granted much insight, but was henceforth burdened with a persisting limp.

The Psalm, ascribed to David, often uses walking, or the paths chosen to walk, as metaphors both for man's struggles and for man's quest for divine guidance. Indeed, symbolic paths are strewn throughout the Psalms. Even the first line of the first Psalm declares: "Happy is the man who has not followed the course of the wicked or taken the path of the sinners."

There are additional psalmic lines such as: "O Lord, lead me along your righteous path," or, "My feet have held to your path," or, "You have let me stride on freely; my feet have not slipped," or, "He guides me in the right path." And for those neglectful of a path of blamelessness there were psalmic phrases such as: "They stumbled with no one to help."

For a nomadic people, ever moving, ever preparing to flee, walking became an irreplaceable daily activity much like eating and sleeping. And the language of their prayer inevitably emphasized that righteousness was not a gift to be plucked idly from the ripened vine, but was a goal to be achieved by walking a path of probity. A sedentary, agricultural people might have chosen other forms of expression for their religious fervor.

But then, after so many plaintive prayers, Psalm 26 appears with the following curious declaration: "I wash my hands in innocence / And walk around Your altar, O Lord / Raising my voice in thanksgiving / And telling all Your wonders."

What meaning might walking around an altar hold? Was it a spontaneous expression of religious exuberance? Or might it hint of something more ancient, perhaps shared by other societies and religions?

The walking around, the circling of an altar (or a sacred tomb or even an entire sanctuary), is a fundamental element of the customs of many older religions. The nomadic Hebrews regularly circumambulated their Holy of Holies. And Muslims, when on their sacred pilgrimage, still walk in processions around the Ka'ba in Mecca, making seven circuits corresponding to the Islamic concept of seven celestial spheres.

Buddhists regularly walk around their *stupas*, those dome-shaped monuments dedicated to Buddha. In Western Europe, newly crowned kings circled their capitol city, in olden days on foot, when assuming control of the realm. And the Chinese emperors regularly circled the Forbidden City in a rite the origins of which preceded the keeping of written records.

In most cultures the circling was clockwise, representing expressions of peaceful reverence. Counterclockwise encirclement, on the other hand, symbolized hostile intent. Celtic warriors drove their chariots in a counterclockwise pathway around enemy strongholds before initiating an attack. In the Book of Joshua: "The Lord said to Joshua, "See, I will deliver Jericho and her king and her warriors into your hands. Let all your troops march around the city and complete one circuit of the city. Do these six days, with seven priests carrying seven rams' horns preceding the Ark. On the seventh day, march around the city seven times, with the priests blowing the horns. And when a long blast is sounded on the horn — as soon as you hear that sound of the horn — all the people shall give a mighty shout. Thereupon the city wall will collapse."

The lame, in all vulnerable societies, were intentionally excluded from assuming any tribal authority, either in the military or the priestly class. And for the wandering Israelites, ceaseless walking through the wilderness of Sinai represented a life-saving capability. Beyond a way of moving the vulnerable tribes of Israel through the wilderness, walking then became symbolic of many things. It sanctified their altars, it provided them with imagery for prayers, and it even hastened the destruction of hostile strongholds such as Jericho.

Ritual walking, in circumambulating sacred sites and enemy fortresses, as well as in the ancient Jewish ritual of marriage, became a way of achieving unity with that which was being encircled. In one Jewish tradition, the bride circles the groom seven times under the *chuppah* before the wedding ceremony commences. And while she circles, the groom prays. The walls, which separate bride and groom, will fall and their souls will then be indivisibly united.

From Afros to *payes,* hair matters

Long before there had been any rational understanding of how the body functioned, primitive peoples were readily assigning elaborate purposes and attributes to human organs. Some explanations were credible, but most were outlandish.

Among the more ridiculous was the notion that the heart was the source of human compassion, tenderness and romantic feelings; that the liver generated either courage or, alternatively, cowardice; and that the intestines were the source of fortitude and endurance. On the other hand, skeletal muscle was justifiably believed to be the source of strength; and hair was cited as the tissue from which males derived virility, long life and vigor.

Hair is mentioned in the Hebrew Bible, sometimes as a visible symbol of an unblemished body as in the case of David's son Absalom, or sometimes as a metaphor for feminine beauty. But to the prophets, hair represented more profound, primal emotions.

To Isaiah, a head shorn of hair signified defeat on the battlefield, a loss of arrogance, a return to humble status. To Ezra, hair was the vehicle wherein intense grief was exhibited: "I tore hair out of my head and beard, and I sat desolate."

And Jeremiah, when describing a suitable punishment for the profane ones who ignored the bidding of the Lord, declared, "Shear their locks and cast them away."

And then there was Samson, of the tribe of Dan. He was a judge of the Israelites who had served faithfully for 20 years and was endowed with immense strength and courage. It was said that this strength was in his hair. But then Samson chose to visit Gaza, where he took up with a fair harlot, Delilah.

At the secret bidding of the Philistines, she sought to discover the true origins of Samson's strength. Only after much seductive persuasion did Samson finally reveal the source of his great powers. And so, while he slept, Delilah summoned the Philistines who sheared off Samson's hair, which was in the form of seven braids. Shorn of hair, and thus shorn of power, Samson could then be subdued and blinded. During his imprisonment, some of his hair grew back, sufficient for him to use his regenerated strength to destroy the temple of Dagon, his captors and himself.

There are few cultures that have not assigned the source of physical prowess and sexual potency to hair. Even cultures far removed from the Mediterranean region have concluded that hair was endowed with inherent energy. Certain indigenous tribes of North America believed that when an enemy warrior's hair was removed by scalping, the strength of the vanquished was then transferred to the victor.

To insure the safety and prosperity of his nation, T'ang, the great warrior of an ancient Chinese Empire, decided to sacrifice himself upon the temple altar. After due consideration, however, he instead placed samples of his hair on the altar as a surrogate offering of his power. In ancient China, sword-crafting artisans added locks of their hair to the smelting furnace, as a symbolic sacrifice of themselves, to guarantee the bravery and effectiveness of their swords.

Amongst the heathen tribes living at the northern borders of the Roman Empire, only kings, their sons and certain military leaders were permitted to allow their hair to go uncut. The Romans, who decried unruly hair, called these barbarian enemies, *Gallia comata* (the hairy Gauls).

As a sign of total humility before a higher spiritual authority, novitiate monks in many Christian orders shaved off their hair, thus creating a characteristic circular tonsure. Over the centuries, many corporeal parts of deceased saints have been preserved and venerated by the faithful, particularly samples of their hair. On designated days, some churches proudly display a lock of their patron saint's hair, typically encased in a jeweled container. And to this day, the parents of European children make a major ceremony of their son's first haircut. It is common practice for the mother to preserve the first shorn locks in a small locket.

There is, of course, some basis for connecting luxuriant growth of hair with physical strength and sexual virility. It is no endocrinological secret that sexual maturity in the adolescent male coincides with the appearance of facial and body hair. Excessive body hair in the male is called hypertrichosis, and represents little more than a genetic variant with no clinical significance. However, when there is excessive coarse hair in a woman, it is called hirsutism (from a Latin word meaning shaggy), and it presents a diagnostic challenge to the clinician. Certain medications such as dilantin may cause this hirsutism. In rare cases it represents an external manifestation of the adrenal or ovarian tissues.

Men and women can react differently to the same agent; prolonged starvation, for example, may cause excessive body hair in women. Women survivors of concentration camps had often observed increased facial hair. Starved male prisoners, on the other hand, noted the reverse, namely, a loss of facial hair.

An abundance of hair, in most cultures, presages longevity, strength and virility. But some have also used hairstyling to express their personal beliefs and establish their identities. This might take the form of an Afro haircut, dreadlocks, pigtails, or even an intentionally shaved head. In observance of the instruction declared in Leviticus 19:27: "Ye shall not round the corners of your head." Orthodox Jewish males have allowed their side earlocks, the *payes,* to grow unshorn. Leo Rosten remembers that a street in Brooklyn inhabited by many Chasidic Jews was frequently called *Rue de la Pais.*

A house divided, dispersed and lost

Explorer Lewis told to look for traces of Lost Tribes of Israel

During his presidency, Thomas Jefferson authorized an expedition to explore the western reaches of the Missouri River waterways from its confluence with the Mississippi and then to verify the existence of further navigable waterways, from the mountainous watersheds of the Rockies to the Pacific Ocean.

To command such an enterprise, which he called "A Voyage of Discovery," Jefferson selected Merriwether Lewis, his private secretary, and a former captain in the U.S. Army, and he chose William Clark, a fellow Army officer, as co-leader of the expedition.

Lewis was instructed to gather anthropological information from the Native Americans he met, such as age at which menstruation began and ended, what were their remedies for various afflictions, whether there were sacrificed animals in their religious rites, and whether they possessed ardent spirits (alcohol). He was also told to ask the following question: "What affinity exists between their religious ceremonies and those of the Jews?"

This question about Jewish customs incorporated into Shoshone rituals would seem bizarre were it not for the fact that many Christians were then obsessed with the thought that the so-called 10 Lost Tribes of Israel might turn up in one or another part of the globe. It was a common practice, then, to instruct those about to embark on a voyage into the exotic wilderness to seek out these lost Israelites. Missionaries to the African interior, such as Dr. David Livingstone, for example, considered a search for the Lost Tribes as essential to their spiritual agenda. For highly educated physicians such as those working with Lewis, it was therefore quite natural to seek evidence of an Israelite texture within Native American culture.

Lewis departed Washington on July 5, 1803, traveled to Pittsburgh, assumed command of a 55-foot keelboat and sailed down the Ohio River, picking up Clark in Louisville, Kentucky.

They returned to the eastern states in 1806 with no evidence that any of the encountered Native American tribes might be descended from the Israelites.

And what of these Lost Tribes? History tells us that after the death of Solomon and during the reign of Jeroboam, the 12 Hebrew tribes divided into two kingdoms, Judah in the south, populated by the tribes of Judah and Benjamin, adhering to the Davidic traditions; and Israel in the north, peopled by the remaining 10 tribes of Reuben, Simeon, Levi, Issachar, Zebullun, Dan, Naphtali, Gad, Asher and Joseph.

In the year 722 BCE, King Shalmaneser V of Assyria conquered Israel and exiled the 10 northern tribes to the upper reaches of Mesopotamia. There is no evidence of any substantial return of these exiled tribes to Samaria or the other provinces of Israel. It has been assumed that the enslaved Israelites were gradually assimilated into the local citizenry, losing their religious and ethnic identity (although a few enclaves in the mountainous Kurdish regions did preserve their Hebraic customs and beliefs).

Some have nurtured the belief that somehow these 10 tribes have survived and exist today in some as yet unexplored region of the world. Others claim that the Khazars of southern Russia were descended from the 10 tribes; yet others contend that the lost tribes were ancestors of the Anglo-Saxon hordes. Still others declare that the Lost Tribes are alive and well in Ethiopia. Among some Jews there prevails the plaintive hope that the 10 Lost Tribes may yet be found and reunited with their cousins, the descendants of the tribes of Judah and Benjamin. They recall the words of the prophet Ezekiel: "Behold I will take the children of Israel...and will gather them on every side, and bring them into their land. And they shall be divided into two kingdoms no more."

From Pharaoh on down, 7 is the magic number

Pharaoh had a troubling dream. He dreamt of seven well-nourished cows rising from the Nile, followed in time by seven malnourished cows, which then consumed the seven healthy cows.

None of Pharaoh's advisors could interpret this bewildering dream about sevens; and so, on the advice of his cupbearer, Pharaoh summoned Joseph, a servant of the chief steward, who was reputed to be wise in understanding the underlying messages within dreams. Joseph, 31 centuries before Sigmund Freud, translated the dream to explain the imminence of seven bountiful years to be followed by seven years of want.

Consider how often the number seven arises in the Jewish Bible. In Genesis, the world was created in six days, but its creator rested on the seventh.

During the siege of Jericho, the Israelites were instructed to eat only unleavened bread for seven days. Seven priests with seven trumpets, on the seventh day of the siege, circled the enemy fortress seven times, and Jericho then fell.

During the siege of Jericho, the Israelites were instructed to eat only unleavened bread for seven days. Seven priests with seven trumpets, on the seventh day of the siege, circled the enemy fortress seven times, and Jericho then fell.

Not merely the seventh day, but the seventh year was selected as the interval of rest when the fields were left fallow, debts erased and slaves freed.

Jesse's rod had seven spirits. Solomon devoted seven years to the construction of his great temple in Jerusalem. And there were seven heavens with seven orders of angels. The leper called Naaman was cleansed of his disease only after he had bathed in the waters of the Jordan River seven times. Indeed, the numeral seven is mentioned 77 times in the Bible.

In the Book of Proverbs, we learn; "Wisdom hath built her house and hewn out seven pillars." And seven pillars has remained a metaphor for abiding wisdom.

An angel asked Zechariah, the prophet, what he saw. Zechariah responded by describing a golden lamp stand with seven branches: the lamps fed by the yield of two olive trees. Thus did he describe the *menorah*, a Hebrew word meaning giver of light. (The Arabic word "minaret," a slender tower associated with a mosque, is derived from the same root.) In Christian cathedrals, the seven-branched candelabras are sometimes referred to as the Jesse lamp stands, an allusion to Jesse's family tree that included both David and Jesus.

Seven is a deeply revered number in many faiths. In Islam, for example, there are seven holy imams in each era. And in their pilgrimage to Mecca, the faithful circumambulate the inner shrine seven times. In addition, there are seven wondrous gates to paradise.

In Morocco, wives who have not borne children follow an ancient custom. They wrap their girdles securely seven times around a special tree.

In the ancient belief systems, the Egyptians honored the numeral seven as the symbol of eternal life. There were seven gates to Thebes.

The Greco-Roman god Apollo was worshipped on the seventh day of each month. There were seven Hesperides (the nymphs of ancient Greece). And seven strings to the classical lyre. Rome had seven wise masters, as did Greece.

And when, in the second century of the Common Era, Antipater decided to compile the great wonders of the world, he identified seven of them. Nor can we ignore the seven continents and the seven seas.

Rites of initiation, whether into military units or into certain professions, are common to all cultures. The transition from careless childhood to a world of adult responsibilities is often marked by solemn ceremony. In some animistic societies there is even a ritual with the symbolic death of the child and his rebirth as an adult. Sometimes this transformation is accompanied with trials by fire or the need to complete certain hazardous and brave deeds.

Often these dangerous tasks are seven in number, sometimes symbolized as seven successive rungs of a golden ladder.

In some cultures, each of the seven stages of initiation represents one of the seven heavenly bodies. Even Shakespeare visualized the lives of men and women in seven stages: "All the world's a stage…and one man in his time plays many parts, his acts being in seven stages."

Hippocrates, who fought to remove medicine from the realm of superstition, nonetheless found something appealing in the number seven. "Through its hidden properties, the number seven maintains all things in being, bestows life and motion, and its influence extends to heavenly things," he wrote. But to the later sages of medicine, seven was not a particularly critical numeral. There are no seven cardinal signs of prognostic significance, no seven essential medications or even seven fundamental diseases, in the great texts of medicine.

People have a peculiar fascination with numbers expressed in this strange institution called numerology. Numbers, some believe, hold hidden powers and cryptic messages that extend far beyond their arithmetical values; messages which only the select may interpret. When gamblers are free to select a lottery number, seven is selected more frequently than any other single digit. And seven, much to the dismay of the inveterate gambler, holds a special significance in dice.

From the holiest of shrines to the most secular of gambling casinos, the magisterial number seven remains special and cherished.

Nor can they do any good

U ntil this past century, the practice of medicine offered little beyond the occasional relief of pain, a few nostrums, and some primitive surgical interventions. The average adult in the ancient kingdom of Judah therefore had few choices when confronted with serious illness in himself or in his family. He could accept the grim realities with a quiet stoicism, declaring his humility before divine judgment; he could employ whatever medical facilities that were then available, or, in desperation, he could resort to the arcane methods used by his neighbors.

> *It was said that many Jews carried amulets containing fragments of parchment with written prayers against the onset of pestilence.*

An incantation is generally defined as a chanting of a sequence of words alleged to possess magical properties, to be used after the onset of illness. A talisman is a stationary object purporting to have magical powers. It served as a preventive measure against a threat of illness or to ward off malign forces. An amulet, on the other hand, is a portable charm, usually worn around the neck, and is specifically designed to ward off future evil.

The ancient Egyptians had declared that the beetle was holy and they routinely wore its shell, the scarab, as a protective amulet. Post-exilic Judaic culture had been deeply embedded within the folklore of the Middle East and accordingly there were no Talmudic injunctions forbidding Jews from wearing amulets. It was said that many Jews carried amulets containing fragments of parchment with written prayers against the onset of pestilence.

Deuteronomy (6:4-9), when discussing the reverence to be accorded to its laws and rules, declares: "Bind them for a sign upon your hand and let them serve as a symbol on your forehead; inscribe them on the doorpost of your house and upon your gates." Thus was born the custom of attaching an encapsulated fragment of Holy Scripture to the right doorpost of one's home. The *mezuzah* can probably be construed as a talisman, but only if it is regarded solely as a magical contrivance rather than as a reminder to abide by holy commandments. Deuteronomy does not provide incantations or secret devices to ward off impending illnesses.

It is easy to condemn the citizens of ancient Jerusalem who resorted in desperation to superstitious practices to ward off evil. Perhaps if they had had access to modern medicine, they might not have sought out idolatrous measures. And it might be well to remember how many observant, well-educated folk in this enlightened era still carry lucky charms around their necks. Let he who is without a lucky number or a lucky item cast the first stone.

Rabbi Akiba ben Joseph (C 50 - 135 CE) was once asked, "We both know in our hearts that there is no truth in idolatry. Nevertheless, do we not see people enter a shrine and come out cured?" The learned rabbi responded by declaring that the illness which prompted the visit to the idolatrous shrine might have been destined to depart, coincidentally on that very day. Should God now punish this foolish supplicant by intentionally extending his affliction a few more days? Being a fool is enough punishment. Rabbi Akiba was thus showing a profound respect for the laws of nature rather than the miracles of idolatry.

'Kein ein hora!' Warding off the evil eye

There was a time in the distant past when curses were taken more seriously. Centuries ago, a person cursed with the full expectation that his invective was more than a hasty expression of wrath or frustration. In the Middle Ages a curse was viewed by both the cursor and the cursed as a palpable threat; and it was generally accepted that properly worded curses could cause herds of cattle to sicken, pregnant women to miscarry, strong men to waste away and even great empires to crumble.

In some belief systems curses ranked high on the rosters of potential causes of human disease. And just as the administration of placebos might convince the credulous soul to feel cured, so too might a grimly delivered curse persuade a believing person to retreat from radiant health to sickness.

The student of cursing must distinguish carefully among expletive profanities, denunciations, oaths, swearing, spells, voodoo, whammies, incantations, solemn damnation and maledictions, all of which are sometimes called curses. Of course, not all curses were designed expressly to affect another person's health. Curses, after all, are of many sizes and missions: Some may be short-lived, others may endure for generations; some are casually rendered, others solemn; some are narrowly focused while others are broadly indiscriminate. The social standing of the one delivering it enhances the ultimate success of a curse. A curse intoned by a bearded rabbi would probably be more effective than one uttered by an itinerant peddler.

Cursing, more as an insult than a malevolent wish, was institutionalized in Elizabethan England. It consisted of two or more belittling adjectives modifying a demeaning noun. The curse was even more effective if the chosen words were alliterative, i.e., "You are a fawning, festering flapdragon." Note that this form of curse, common to the Shakespearean plays, assumed that the cursee already was a victim of some terrible malady and that the curse accomplished little more than announcing something that was a pre-existing reality. In general, the more flamboyant the curse, the less malign was its effect. Indeed, some such curses were so heavily laden with hyperbole, so excessively wordy, that they generated more amusement than fear.

Ireland, a land where poetry and curses are taken seriously, improved upon the Elizabethan style of cursing. The Hibernian curses have wit, color and originality. A favorite is, "Do you realize that you are depriving a village somewhere of an idiot?" Yiddish curses cover a nearly infinite variety of insults, in fine shades of meaning: *shlemiel, shlimazel, shmendrik* – similar but not quite the same.

Eastern European Jews, from centuries of oppression, developed a unique variety of curses which were plaintive rather than vindictive, elliptical rather than blunt, and often poignantly humorous. "May a little child be named after you." (Said in a culture where children were named only after the deceased.) "May you die and come back as a candelabrum to hang by day and burn by night." "May onions grow out of your navel."

When a curse begins with the word may ("May you be brought low by leprosy"), it implies that the victim of the curse does not currently have leprosy. Thus, the curse carries a tacit measure of uncertainty, an interval of time between the wish and the emergence of the disease, allowing for a countervailing cottage industry to spring up, namely those who, for a fee, provided incantations to neutralize the impending effects of the original curse.

As a protective shield against the possibility of a curse taking effect upon her child, an Eastern European Jewish mother might exclaim "*Kein ein hora!*" (May no evil eye bring harm to him.)

The "may" curse, spoken by struggling humans, contrasts sharply with scriptural curses proclaimed by the Lord: "I will send pestilence among you and you shall be delivered into enemy hands. The Lord will strike you with consumption, fever...madness, blindness and dismay." (Deut. 28). Note that there is no "may," no latent interval, no ambiguity in curses of divine origin.

The dynamics of cursing leave many questions unresolved. Does the person being cursed have to hear the curse in order for it to become effective? Do curses carry something akin to statutes of limitation or do they operate forever? Do curses function even if they are directed against someone innocent of the crime which had provoked the original curse? What is the source of the power invoked to translate a curse to a real hazard? And finally, why, in this imperfect world, are there more curses than blessings?

Dr. Ludwig Lazarus Zamenhof of Lithuania created
what he considered a universal language, Esperanto.

From Yiddish to Esperanto, in one easy step

A New York University professor of linguistics, Howard Schollman, has recently declared that Hebonics is a legitimate second language which deserves serious recognition along with the other *patois* and tongues so common in multilingual communities. And, in 2005 the New York City school board also accepted Hebonics, sometimes called Jewish English, as an officially sanctioned second language.

> *'Mountains, shmountains, you want maybe I should get a nose-bleed?'*

So what is Hebonics? It is a variety of kitchen English, largely confined to the United States, which employs virtually no non-English vocabulary, but incorporates a distinctively Yiddish texture to its syntax. Thus Hebonics has its own characteristic phraseology and tortured grammar which typically constructs answers in the form of questions and inverts the positioning of the objects, verbs and subjects within the sentence sequence. Hebonics, as an ethnically-associated variant form of English, also manages to convey the low-level anxieties and pervasive skepticism of first-generation Jewish Americans who are not yet convinced that they are as fully American as their neighbors of Celtic origin. The language embodies, as well, the bittersweet nuances of Yiddish, the veneer of cynicism and the essence of convoluted Jewish humor. Words are sometimes repeated in Hebonics but with a characteristic *shm* prefix added to the repeated word; (influenza, shminfluenza, as long as you're healthy). Clearly, though, Hebonics is not Yiddish, but is nonetheless Yiddish in spirit without using any Yiddish words.

What are examples of Hebonics? A son telephones his mother after a moderately lengthy interval:

Son: "How are you, Mother?"

Mother: "Dead I'm not but wouldn't you maybe want to know sometimes?"

Or: Son: "Would you like a vacation in the Catskill Mountains?"

Mother: "Mountains, shmountains, you want maybe I should get a nose-bleed?"

Languages come in all forms and degrees of duration. Beyond the current languages with their formal vocabularies, phonologies, grammars, syntaxes and literature, there are some classical languages which are still immensely influential but, like Latin, are spoken only by small enclaves of people such as the Roman Catholic clergy. Then there are language variants (sometimes called *lingua francas*), tongues which extend beyond the territories of dialects, cants, jargons and argots, to include such accretive languages as Caribbean Creole, pidgin English, Cockney English, Ladino and Yiddish (which is a grammatically rudimentary language blended of elements of low German, Hebrew, Polish, Russian, Lithuanian and, increasingly, English).

Finally, there are languages which have been intentionally assembled to fill a specific purpose, much like the argots of the underworld or the cants of certain professions. One of these synthetic languages, called Esperanto, has achieved a small measure of endurance. It was exposed to the world about 119 years ago and still has about five million people who use it as a secondary language.

Esperanto was created by a Jewish physician while practicing ophthalmology in Warsaw. Ludwig Lazarus Zamenhof, of Lithuanian extraction, was born in 1859 in the ethnically diverse city of Bialystok, then part of Czarist Russia. Bialystok was populated by a mixture of Lithuanians, Jews, Poles, Russians and Germans. Therefore, mercantile negotiations with the region required a working knowledge of at least a few of these tongues.

Zamenhof's father and grandfather were both professional translators, but young Ludwig's intense interest in languages was less materially oriented. He envisaged a grammatically simple language which might transcend ethnic and national insularity, diminish estrangements between peoples, rise above linguistic nationalism and ultimately offer harmony to its speakers rather than condone bigotry. His first attempts to simplify Latin and make it more alive failed, and he concluded that only an entirely artificial language, free of idiosyncrasies such as complex declensions, might answer his needs.

Zamenhof's family sent him to Moscow to study medicine, but even during his matriculation he continued his efforts at creating a global language. By the 1880s young Zamenhof had established a prosperous practice in eye disease in Warsaw but his alternate interest in linguistics prevailed, and in 1887 he published his first monograph on his new language. For whatever reason, he refrained from signing his name. Instead he employed the pseudonym *Medicus Esperanto* in Latin, "The Hopeful Doctor." The followers of his language then chose Esperanto as the appropriate name for Zamenhof's international language.

A feverish need to measure

The simple clinical thermometer remains one of medicine's most enduring instruments. It is likely that this fragile cylinder of glass yields more utilitarian information than any other portable piece of diagnostic medical equipment. Certainly no Jewish home is regarded as completely furnished without at least one thermometer in a drawer.

Fever, said Galen, is the scream of deep illness seeking attention. And to the ancients, fever had always been the herald of systemic illness. Older medical texts created an elaborate menu of fever profiles. There were fevers called eruptive (coincident with the appearance of rashes), remitting, cerebral (associated with stupor or coma), relapsing, quotidian (daily) and hectic (associated with delirium), to name a few.

When fever rages and the pulse accelerates, a measuring instrument like a thermometer is not really required. Many a Jewish mother from an older generation will tell you that her hand upon a fevered brow is more sensitive than any objective instrument. But might there be trifling increments of fever, low grade, perhaps, that not even a grandmother's hand could detect?

One of the earliest questions demanding an answer was whether there was such a thing as a normal human temperature. To determine this, the thermometer would have to be scaled. The ancient Greek scientists talked freely of heat and cold but assigned no numeric value to either. To them it was sufficient to note that one object was warmer or cooler than another. Galen, more quantitatively oriented, suggested four levels of temperature, with a midpoint being a fresh mixture of boiling water and ice.

By the 17th century, physics had evolved to a degree where heat had to be calibrated; and scientists interested in both the weather and human illness sought ways of quantifying it.

What characteristics should a heat-measuring instrument possess? It must respond quickly and consistently to temperature changes in its surrounding environment. It must also possess some sort of scale, thus providing the observer with a numeric value which is consistent and meaningful. A reading on one thermometer must be the same as a reading on another, tested at the same time, on the same patient.

The first thermometers were based on two well-known physical phenomena: First, that the volume of liquid or gas expands with increasing heat, and second, that warm objects transfer some of their heat to neighboring cold objects until they reach the same (equilibrating) temperature.

The invention of a reliable thermometer began with an obscure Venetian physician, Santorio Santorre, professor of medicine at the medical school in Padua. In 1611, he devised a simple instrument consisting of an air-filled globe which was inserted vertically into an open container of dye-stained water. This ponderous apparatus was wheeled to the bedside and the globe placed within the armpit of the patient. When the globe was warmed by the human body, its contained air absorbed some of the heat and then expanded, thus displacing some of the water at the end of the globe. This instrument was crude and certainly not mobile; nor could it provide a precise, quantitative temperature reading, but it was a beginning.

Later in the 17th century, the Royal Society of London accepted the challenge of trying to assemble a gadget to measure temperature. Many of its members, including Wren, Halley and Boyle, devoted time to this task. Their instruments were based on Santorre's principle that heat causes gases or fluids to expand – the more the heat, the more the expansion. They recognized, too, that the fluid to be used should not freeze easily nor should it be colorless. Hence they replaced the fluid in their experimental instruments with wine (which is why the earlier instruments were called spirit thermometers).

Then came Daniel Fahrenheit, who was born in Danzig but lived much of his life in Holland as an instrument-maker. It was he who devised the instrument consisting of a glass rod with a very thin inner bore and a small reservoir below filled with liquid mercury. As the mercury-filled bulb was warmed, the contained mercury expanded and the mercury column rose within the tube. His instrument was calibrated so that the freezing point of water was placed at 32 degrees and the boiling point was 212 degrees. Andre Celcius, a Swedish astronomer, suggested that the freezing point should be at 100 degrees and the boiling point at zero. His friend, the Swedish botanist-physician

Carl Linnaeus, felt that this was counter-intuitive and suggested rather that the warmer the object being tested, the higher should be the scale number. Celcius accepted this and the modern Celsius scale, with the zero denoting the freezing point of water and the 100 signifying the boiling point, is now the standard system of thermometric notation.

The old-fashioned glass thermometer needed no batteries to be replaced, no engineering degrees to assemble and no expensive outlays to purchase. It was simple and reliable and its only failing was its fragility and the constant anxiety that a child, thinking it might be a candy stick, might bite it. But whether it was the classical thermometer or the more sophisticated temperature-quantifying machine, most American families still use it as the sole criterion of health and sickness in their children.

Many an American child, in the early stage of an upper-respiratory infection, has prayed that the thermometer will read above the normal value so that he may stay home from school.

A cherished day to remember

The great jazz musician, Louis Armstrong, had always claimed that he was born on the Fourth of July, 1900. Historians, more interested in tangible records than romantic recollections, have finally located his baptismal records showing that he had been born on Aug. 4, 1901. Uncaring realism has replaced congenial sentimentality.

A great performer of Irish descent, George M. Cohan, was truly born on the Fourth of July in Providence; and when he wrote his famous signature song, he exploited this with the key phrase, "I'm a Yankee Doodle Dandy, born on the Fourth of July!" Others in the entertainment world born on July 4th include Gina Lollabrigida, Virginia Graham, Geraldo Rivera, Eva Marie Saint, Gloria Stuart and Mitch Miller. If birthdays are distributed somewhat randomly, then about one out of each 365 persons should be celebrating his/her birthday on the same day that this nation commemorates its origins. And it should not come as a surprise, therefore, when a handful of people are said to be born on July 4th.

The Declaration of Independence had been completed, duly signed and openly proclaimed on the 4th of July. This day assumed unique significance, particularly for the American patriots who had supported and signed it on behalf of their respective states. Thomas Jefferson, the third president and author of this Declaration, considered it to be the most important event in his lifetime. He died on July 4, 1826 – exactly 50 years to the day after the signing of the Declaration. And in New England, his long-time rival and late-in-life friend John Adams, the second president, also died on July 4, 1826. The fifth president of the United States, James Monroe, similarly died on the 4th of July in 1831. The concurrence of these deaths on the 4th of July may be an astonishing coincidence. More likely, though, it represents a compelling example of a phenomenon that has been noted by demographers: Namely, the ability of a dying person to delay the moment, even day, of death so that it might coincide with a date of great personal significance, a day such as one's birthday.

For those who are the beneficiaries of that precious independence affirmed by the Declaration, whether they be presidents or anonymous American citizens, July 4 must therefore hold a singular importance; important enough to make them think, wishfully perhaps, that they had in fact been born on that special date; or, as a more dramatic homage to July 4, by keeping themselves alive when mortally ill until that date had arrived.

Stark realities have often tempered the degree to which Jews have allowed themselves to be sentimental. But there are certain dates, both secular and holy, which rarely go unremembered by Jews. The tenets of the High Holy Days may or may not be strictly observed but these special days of awe are rarely totally forgotten.

Birthdays, even wedding anniversaries, are sometimes forgotten. No one, however, forgets the 4th of July since it is a national holiday marked by many public celebrations. The birth of this nation is certainly to be honored although dying on the 4th of July would be considered by some to be a grossly excessive display of patriotism. Adams, Jefferson and Monroe were (by 19th- century standards) already elderly and the Fourth to them was substantially more than a time for barbecues and fireworks.

Being born on the 4th of July, however, is another matter. One does not plan the date of one's own birth. And therefore to be born on the 4th must signify a special benefaction, a gift marking the newborn as uniquely privileged. Ask a sampling of American adults this question: "What day of the year would you like your birthday to fall on?" And an inordinate number will say: "The 4th of July or the 25th of December."

At least three explanations might account for this startling concentration of Jewish births on the 4th of July. First, that many of the Jews born in the villages of Eastern Europe were divinely preordained to be born on a day sacred to the citizens of a distant nation. Since it was unlikely that 19th-century Jews living in *shtetls* even knew the significance of the Fourth, or that they might on some future day flee to America, makes this an implausible explanation. Second, that it represents a statistical artifact since, with a limited sample, any date might have shown a preponderance by chance alone; and that if the sample had been much larger, this clustering of births on the 4th of July would have disappeared. And third, the most reasonable explanation, that the clustering represents a bit of wishful thinking.

Consider how the information recorded on death certificates is compiled. A distraught relative, let us say a nephew, sits down with a funeral parlor representative and is asked a series of 20 or 30 questions, the answers to which are required by law. One of these questions is date of birth of the deceased. In a settled community such as the United States where there are birth certificates, everyone knows his or her birthday. But for a population born in rural czarist Russia, where no communal records had been consistently maintained, the birth date was sometimes unknown, or only dimly recalled. Accordingly, about 10 percent of death certificates of Jews born overseas have a question mark in the box requesting the birthdate.

In other instances the respondent (in this case our hypothetical nephew) recalls the month and year but not the specific date. Now, place yourself in the position of this living relative when asked for the birthday of his Uncle David. You remember that it was some day early in July, in the year 1889. And so, in response to the question, you then blurt out, "July 4, 1889." It was not a deliberate or even a conscious lie. It was located, you knew, somewhere in early July; and it could have been the Fourth. And what greater way of validating Uncle David's love of this nation then by proclaiming him a Yankee Doodle Dandy, born on the 4th of July?

We happily accept the inordinate number of Jews of an older generation said to be born on that most American of days, July Fourth, acknowledging that it represents little more than some wishful thinking encouraged by a touch of authentic patriotism.

Made in the USA
San Bernardino, CA
26 January 2014